THE
NEW ONLINE
TEACHING GUIDE

*A Training Handbook of
Attitudes, Strategies and
Techniques for the
Virtual Classroom*

Ken W. White, Ph.D.

This book was previously published by: Pearson Education, Inc.

Between the time Website information is gathered and published, some site may have closed. Also, the transcription of URLs can result in typographical errors. The author would appreciate notification where these occur so that they may be corrected in subsequent editions.

Internet: white_kenw@msn.com

ISBN 978-1-4357-0146-5

Printed in the United States of America

CONTENTS

Preface

The New Online Teaching Guide: A Training Handbook of Attitudes, Strategies and Techniques for the Virtual Classroom continues the purpose of the original edition—to respond to the questions posed by new and seasoned online teachers, to place them at ease in their jobs and to get them started effectively in the online classroom. The idea for the first book came in 1995 from the growing need across the nation for teachers with the specific attitudes and skills for the online environment. In the past twelve years, the number of college and university courses offered to students via the Internet and Web has increased exponentially. Numerous colleges and universities throughout the country are establishing distance learning programs with online courses facilitated through various types of conferencing software.

Today, online is part of a new educational culture with its own distinct characteristics. Although not a panacea for educational change or reform, online education offers an important alternative. Like Zachary Karabell recognizes in his recent book, *What's College For? The Struggle to Define American Higher Education*, no one model, either traditional or online education, can possibly meet the needs of a system that encompasses 3,500 separate schools, millions of teachers, tens of millions of students and billions of dollars. But online education does fill a niche in the changing nature of education in this country. Consequently, many traditional educators have made the transition to the online medium. Unfortunately, they do not always have the necessary skills to perform online teaching responsibilities effectively.

The feasibility for this project was partly researched by my attendance at the Eighth Annual Meeting of the Western Cooperative for Educational Telecommunications in San Francisco in 1996. The Western Cooperative serves its members as a central clearinghouse for information and contacts; planner and facilitator of multi state projects; "spokesperson" to campus, state and federal policy makers; provider of user support services; and evaluator and researcher on educational uses of telecommunications and information technologies. The theme of the conference was "Education in the Virtual Age." I offered a preview of the book and asked the audience for feedback about the idea. The message was clear: the 20-30 distance educators who attended the presentation expressed a strong interest. They saw the book as a much-needed training resource for the expanding opportunities in the field of electronically mediated learning.

As a result, the original edition, *The Online Teaching Guide,* was published by Pearson Education in 2000. The collection of essays was authored by University of Phoenix Online Campus faculty members with over one hundred years of collective teaching experience, and contained ideas that were developed, tested and refined in hundreds of online classrooms. The book was intended as a practical introduction for instructors, beginning or otherwise, who wanted useful ideas and techniques that would help them teach more effectively in the online classroom. It was not meant as a *technical* guide, but as a valuable resource for thinking through conceptual issues and developing effective online instructional techniques. It assumed that its readers were thoughtful individuals committed to enhancing their teaching in the online and "onsite" environments, and capable of judging how the concepts and suggestions applied to their own situations. It offered help for online teachers to work their way through the recurring problems, challenges and dilemmas they inevitably face in the virtual classroom.

The first edition also intended to help reduce the feelings of isolation that all teachers experience at some time or another, but particularly prevalent with online instructors, by offering a unique perspective about the online medium. Instead of focusing on approaches that see online teaching as essentially the transmission of information through technology—a sort of "correspondence model" if you will—the book presented attitudes, strategies and techniques that are *socially* based. Online education is an inherently relational and human process, not reducible to sending and receiving electronic messages.

This 2008 edition of *The New Online Teaching Guide* is a training handbook that offers practical tips on how to improve online communication and instructional skills, and recognizes that there is more to effective online teaching than simply the online medium. Online education is not just an electronic way for students to buy their credits, to do their work at home, to study in isolation and occasionally to communicate with their instructor. The book's contributors continue to show how the online medium is not only an irresistible mechanism for learning, but a way of relating to other human beings as well. It reflects a common experience—the virtual university remains a social system consisting of interdependent people, events and behaviors.

The social emphasis of this guide remains poignant. A study from Carnegie Mellon University suggested users of the Internet become lonely and socially withdrawn. "The more people were online, the more signs they gave of being a little bit more socially isolated," said Robert Kraut, the lead author of the study. That is why *The New Online Teaching Guide* suggests that online education requires a value-added approach. Teachers should use technology to enhance the complex private and social activities that make up the learning process. From this perspective, the online classroom exists to be evoked anytime, anywhere, by any learner, to facilitate social interaction and learning. Online education remains a social construct where learning—individual and collective—is supported by instructional technology, not the other way around.

Consequently, this book continues to emphasize a basic belief that effective online instruction requires an *interpersonal* approach. In contrast to the correspondence model, online educators can overcome the sense of isolation often experienced by teachers and learners in the virtual world by expanding the definition of interpersonal communication to that world. Many people consider interpersonal communication to be limited to what can happen between two people—husband-wife, parent-child, teacher-student—in mostly "face to face" situations. This book prefers to see it as a label for a type or *quality* of human interaction that can be present in a variety of situations, including the online classroom. Experience shows that online learning is always about dealing with people and that there are attitudes and behaviors that help online educators make "the interpersonal choice."

Good teaching—online or otherwise—means more than relating interpersonally with students. Beyond relational factors, good teaching requires practical classroom management skills and a deep understanding of various instructional methods and techniques. It demands both meaningful reflection on the question of human relations and a systematic approach to the instructional process. Connections made by good teachers are not only held in the human engagement with students, but also in the professional methods of instruction. Teaching is about student learning and deals with establishing conditions for facilitating learning. Although no single instructional practice or strategy is always superior to any other, good instructors must be at least aware of 'best practices"—skills, abilities and preferences—and be encouraged to adopt them.

Likewise, effective online education not only requires human contact; it demands instructional *structure* with aims, objectives, goals and rhythms. The beginning and seasoned teacher must appreciate this prior to effective teaching. It is through structure—the manipulation of time and virtual space—that the online instructor shapes the social and content elements to inform and enhance the learning process. The teacher who has techniques that implement and facilitate structure, such as setting the tone, encouraging class participation, getting the class organized, is more likely to get off to a good start and maintain it. This book illustrates that the effective use of instructional technology requires specific characteristics that empower adult learners and encourage them to assume responsibilities for their own learning. It promotes characteristics such as:

Interaction and Feedback. Online students learn through active engagement with faculty and other students. Online students need to know if their ideas and responses are productive.

Learner Control. Online students, with their busy schedules and work and family responsibilities, need to be able to stop at any time and to re-enter at their convenience. While *synchronous learning* where teachers and students communicate in "real time" offers a high degree of flexibility to many students, *asynchronous learning* offers more choice of where and, above all, when students access learning.

Directions and Help. Online learners require access to guidance. Instructors, other students and software should prompt learners step-by-step through difficult information and activities.

Consistency and Organization. Explicit and consistent organization increases the retention of new material. Summaries, interaction and feedback should organize and provide a synopsis of the material presented. Instructional segments should be short to accommodate "information overload" common in virtual situations. Online learners develop a sense of accomplishment when instruction is divided into module, units and sub-units.

Assessment and Record Keeping. A tracking system should inform online learners of the materials and activities they need to review before proceeding.

These points are supported and emphasized throughout the following chapters. Chapter one through three establish the foundation for readers to appreciate the importance of applying an interpersonal communication perspective to the online medium, while chapters four through nine offer specific and practical ways to incorporate consistency and organization into the online classroom through various forms of direction and help—facilitation, record keeping, preparation and active learning. Chapter ten directs readers to a major challenge of the online world by discussing the reality of virtual conflict. Chapter eleven concludes with a useful approach for assessing online teaching and learning. The organization of these chapters generally moves from "macro" issues about attitudes most needed by pre-service or beginning online instructors to "micro" issues about specific strategies and techniques likely to be of more concern to the practicing online teacher.

Although the book is intended as a practical guidebook, it also shows how theory shapes practice. In his 1990 book, *Scholarship Reconsidered,* Ernest L. Boyer suggests a new way of defining scholarship that takes into account both theory and practice. Boyer argues that the work of educators might be thought of as having four separate, yet overlapping, professional functions—the scholarships of discovery, integration, application and teaching. "Discovery" comes closest to what is meant by research; "integration" means interpreting data for meaning; "application" engages that meaning in practical ways; and "teaching" communicates meaning to others.

As you read through *The New Online Teaching Guide,* you will find valuable scholarship, not necessarily in terms of original research, but in the four other ways. First, it is designed to help you understand and walk yourself through the important landmarks and pathways of the online world. Written by experts in online education, each chapter is full of detailed information about course preparation, basic online teaching skills, techniques, tools and methods.

Second, you will find redundancy, but I encourage you to accept this as intentional and noteworthy. It is an indicator of integration. For example, the importance of "tone" is expressed throughout the book because a positive and supportive tone is a major pattern of effective online teaching.

Third, it provides comprehensive guidance in the application of experience essential to successful online teaching. Although the authors share many themes, they also offer a variety of personal orientations. Each perspective is unique. This will help you reflect on both the breadth of online teaching issues and on the depth of the challenges that confront all online instructors.

Finally, the book is evidence of scholarly teaching. It is a dynamic learning tool containing the kinds of knowledge and techniques that lead to online teaching competence. Online teaching opportunities are appearing daily and *The New Online Teaching Guide* can prepare you for a successful experience.

Please let me know. I will appreciate it if you do. You can email me at: white_kenw@msn.com

Acknowledgements

I thank Bob Weight of Upper Iowa University for initiating the idea for the 2000 edition of this book, the authors for their contributions, and colleagues at Everett Community College for technical support in preparing the original manuscript back in 1999, especially Anita Newman and Cathy Groger.

I thank my past, present and future online students for being great teachers and making this book possible.

Mostly, though, I thank my wife, Holly, for her proofreading skills, and for her love and support despite her fears that I will become a writing recluse.

About the Author and Editor

Ken White holds a M.Ed. from Western Washington University, and a M.A. and Ph.D. from the University of Washington in the areas of curriculum and instruction, and interpersonal communication. He is currently a tenured faculty member at Everett Community College in Washington State, where he teaches education and speech courses, and an adjunct faculty member at Argosy University and Baker College's online programs. Besides curriculum and instruction, and interpersonal communication, his interests include organizational and instructional communication. In the 1990's, he assisted the College of Arts and Sciences at the University of Washington in developing and initiating a nationally recognized training program to improve the performance of undergraduate faculty and teaching assistants. He continues to consult with local community colleges in alternative ways of assessing teaching and learning, including training and facilitating SGIDs or Small Group Instructional Dialogues. Besides *The New Online Teaching Guide,* Ken is co-editor with Jason D. Baker of *The Student Guide to Successful Online Learning,* published by Pearson Education in 2004. He has taught online since 1992, first for the University of Phoenix where he was an Assistant Department Chair for the Department of General Studies at the online campus and a member of the University's Academic Cabinet. He lives with his wife, Holly, his two sons, Nate and Jamieson, and his step-daughter, Sophia in Washington State.

Chapter 1

"FACE TO FACE"
IN THE ONLINE CLASSROOM

Keeping it Interpersonal and Human

by Ken White

Effective online instruction requires both content knowledge and interpersonal skills because the challenges of the online instructor are essentially about human interaction. Although the online environment depends on computer-mediated communication, it involves people in ways that other examples of distance education may not. Unlike technological forms of the "correspondence course" or interactive television programs, online education is structured around the dynamics of human communication and features the traditional equivalents of due dates, study groups and class discussions. While it is an electronic medium for transmitting content; it is also a human arena for the exchange of ideas. As in any social venture, people are imprecise, unclear and unpredictable. But most importantly, because of its special circumstances, it is even more challenging to work through the uncertainties and ambiguities of online communication.

Online teaching depends on effective communication attitudes and behaviors. Many of the frustrations that beginning online instructors experience are directly related to how they perceive—often subconsciously—communication and its relationship to their students. Limited perceptions often direct ineffective online communication behaviors. For example, the online medium of many programs is completely textual. There is the likely assumption on the part of faculty and students that meaning is primarily in the words on the computer screen. Communication with online students can be seen as only a matter of precision or correct grammar. If so, the online classroom becomes a narrow and frustrating place to work through the inherent complexities of all human communication.

Beginning online instructors should be especially prepared to cope with the ambiguities of computer-mediated communication. They will benefit from developing an understanding that meaning is created in the interaction among students—not in the words alone—and that online communication is more than electronic verbal images. It includes all the human qualities of attitudes, feelings and emotions.

This chapter suggests that the preparation of new online instructors should begin with the awareness of how they can choose to be interpersonal in the online classroom. This includes an understanding of how choice is always a part of human communication, particularly in the online classroom. This is critical—over a decade of experience as a communication instructor has shown me that people believe circumstances, situations and other people often force them to communicate one way or another. It is common for people to think they have limited or no choices when it comes to certain communication circumstances, even though they always have the choice to react negatively or respond thoughtfully to things that happen to them and to what other people say and do.

Choice plays a key role in online communication and teaching. It is my hope in this chapter that by looking at the role of choice in communication and by redefining the concept of interpersonal communication, beginning online instructors will be empowered to influence their future communication encounters in the electronic classroom in a positive way.

Mutating Our Metaphors

Developing effective choices in online communication starts with looking at how people perceive communication. For example, people who see communication as *debate* may limit their choices in such a way as to encourage negative arguments or what "onliners" call *flaming*. If people feel they are in a debate, they naturally try to argue and win. Communication does not have to be seen as a debate. In contrast, some people try to see communication in other ways—for example, as a conversation. They appreciate that by seeing communication as a conversation, people put their choices into a broader perspective. If people don't have to win, they are less inclined to argue or flame.

Organizational theorist Karl Weick describes how people's communication behavior is based on guiding metaphors. He uses the phrase *mutate your metaphors* to describe the skill of changing how one views communication. In Weick's sense, *mutate* means change and *metaphor* means the major images people carry around in their hearts and minds to describe communication.

As Weick (1969) points out, guiding metaphors may not be at the conscious level and effort is required to bring them to awareness. To illustrate this, I do an onsite classroom activity where I draw a chalk line on the board that represents what individuals typically identify as a bird or seagull. I then ask the class, "What do you see?" Students immediately respond, "Bird!" "Seagull!" I then ask again, "What do you see?" For a moment, students look confused, but then a hearty soul joins the game and hollers, "Mountains!" Another yells, "A sideways number three!" "Eyebrows!" The responses mount until they sometimes reach fifteen or twenty. (I always know when the students are fully in the game and actively playing with mutating their metaphors. It's at that point that someone screams out a part of the human anatomy.)

This awareness activity shows that people don't always consciously know when they see things one way or another, but they can change their metaphors and perceptions if they are encouraged to try. Awareness and change are important because the misuse of metaphors can lead to personal and professional problems, including in the online teaching environment.

People communicate in the online classroom based on their guiding metaphors and it's important that people analyze those metaphors and their possible consequences. Metaphors can be deeply flawed. If a metaphor represents a narrow, shallow view of communication situation, it can lead to the inability of articulating a careful analysis of problems and to the alienation of people. Again, seeing communication as something like war distorts and limits thoughtful responses. If you expect a war, for instance, you line up all of your communication "weapons" and "attack our opponent." You are definitely not in the state of mind to be open to what the other person has to say or to let down our defenses and disclose some personal information. Common sports metaphors, along with other outmoded image such as military and cowboys, can become obsessive. People and organizations lose the capacity to think and act appropriately because they are trapped subconsciously in an irrelevant and inappropriate system of thought and communication.

As conceptual frameworks in the online classroom, metaphors are either helpful or rooted in an irrelevant past. Online students can be seen as either human beings who use technology to construct their own knowledge and meaning, or empty vessels on the other end of the computer that need to be filled with data. When metaphors are useful, they clarify complex teaching and learning situations by drawing on simpler and less ambiguous images of life. The way people talk and write shapes the way they look at the world and the way they think and the way they teach.

Like Weick observes, a person needs to consciously choose when it is useful to see communication in a different way. Online instructors must mutate their metaphors about communication's specific form in the online classroom and begin seeing interpersonal communication in ways more appropriate to the situation. The next section will discuss an approach for accomplishing this.

Keeping It Interpersonal

One way that online instructors can mutate their metaphors and increase their sense of choice about online communication is by redefining the concept of interpersonal communication. As a metaphor for choosing how to interact with people, interpersonal communication is often considered to be limited to what happens between two people—husband-wife, parent-child, employer-employee, teacher-student—in mostly "face to face" situations. But this perspective is only one way of seeing interpersonal communication. Interpersonal can also be defined as a type or quality of communication that can be present in a variety of situations. As a quality, interpersonal communication happens in various settings—on the phone, through writing, in committees or other groups and even over the computer.

Because the online environment is so technologically dependent, there is a particular need for instructors to mutate their interpersonal metaphor and to think about the quality of online communication. John Stewart, professor, mentor and friend, offers a way with his *Interpersonal—Impersonal Continuum*. This visual tool or metaphor points to the many possibilities for interpersonal communication in the online classroom. It emphasizes that interpersonal communication is not restricted to situations like the number of people or face to face contact, but is a result of the choice one makes in the online environment.

Imagine the continuum:

INTERPERSONAL------------------------------IMPERSONAL

The continuum functions by emphasizing that one may choose to place a communication situation anywhere on the quality spectrum. It is no longer a question of *either* impersonal *or* interpersonal communication, but of degrees. For example, a person may choose to put an online classroom on the interpersonal end of the continuum. The individual moves specific situations left or right along the continuum depending on his or her choice to be more or less interpersonal. No matter what the situation, the Interpersonal—Impersonal Continuum assumes that a person has a choice to be more or less interpersonal.

But on what does the choice depend? How does the individual know if he or she should choose to make online communication more or less interpersonal? What are the specific qualities at each end of the continuum? Stewart (2005) suggests that there are three reasons for making the choice to be more or less interpersonal in our communication situations, all recognizing that communication is dealing with people.

First, one chooses to be more interpersonal in order to focus on what makes the other person unique. An object can be the same as any other object. For example, if I want to put new batteries in my MP3 player so that I can listen to the blues, any batteries will work. Just as any brand computer disk can be properly formatted to work in the computer that I used to write this chapter.

Online students are never interchangeable, even though they seem so if their online instructors allow them to become only letters on a computer screen. As Sproull and Kiesler (1991) observe, computer-based communication creates new social situations. Reminders of other people and conventions for communicating are weak. This *deindividuation* occurs in the online environment because students have anonymity and lack social reminders. In the online class, messages are likely to show less social awareness, politeness and concern for other's individuality. It is easy to understand, then, why online students can treat each other and can be treated by their instructors so impersonally. This practice is never appropriate. They are as different from each other as people in any other social situation. They differ in personal styles and tastes, religious preferences and political views. Although the electronic medium of the online classroom may reduce social awareness, online instructors must move beyond the medium and create opportunities for students to share their unique experiences and traits.

Online instructors can recognize that their students are unique by carefully designing courses, instructional materials and activities that communicate to students that learning fits personal and unique characteristics and skills. Too frequently, instructors do not consider the impact of course design on student learning. Courses are often designed from a technical and efficiency perspective and little attention is given to how the course fits the person. For example, my online students must pose questions as part of their course work. Student-initiated questions add life to a course and students enjoy struggling with issues in which they have a stake or interest.

Second, one chooses to be more interpersonal in order to show respect for a person's ability to think and make choices. Objects do not think like humans do. That is because objects can only be chosen; they cannot choose. Humans are capable of making choices and initiating action. A computer can seem to operate on its own, but it continues to be dependent on choices initiated from the outside. (This second point needs elaboration. Often people who are physically challenged are treated like objects because they don't appear capable of initiating actions. But there is a difference between the movements of objects and the actions of people. Movements are fundamentally reflexive in nature; actions are reflective. Even though people can be limited in movement, they are still capable of initiating actions. People are reflective. The issue is not whether the physically challenged are able to act, but what are the means to communicate those actions.)

Nowhere is thinking more evident than in the textual environment of the online classroom. If writing is thinking, then online students display their thinking throughout the course, illustrating their individual styles and changing attitudes. Online instructors can show recognition for their students' thinking by maintaining high standards of rigor that challenge students and by building opportunities for choice into their online courses. For example, in my own online classes, I am open to student suggestions about changes in the course, either the present course or future courses. As chapter eleven will show, I seek out their thoughts and will often change the content, rhythm or activities of a course in order to respond to their choices.

Online instructors can recognize that their students are thinkers and give them tasks complex enough to challenge them, but simple enough to accomplish. If an assignment is too complex, it is frustrating and not satisfying. If it is too simple, it is boring. Consequently, successfully challenging an online student requires a high level of open communication and feedback between online teachers and students.

Third, one chooses to be more interpersonal in order to pay attention to relevant feelings and to the whole human being. Humans have feelings. This is what distinguishes humans from objects more than anything else does. Stewart has offered this example. If you kick a rock, you could probably predict what would happen. If you had information on such things as force, velocity, momentum and energy, you might even be able to predict exactly where the rock would end up after you kicked it. But try kicking a person. What will be the human reaction? Will the person cry, look surprised, get angry, or kick you back? You take your chances with the human factor because emotions and feelings can't be measured and calculated. Sure, a person's brain waves, heart rate, pulse, respiration are measured, but that's not the whole person. How people react emotionally to the experiences and events of their lives continues to be immeasurable.

Likewise, the online classroom is an emotional environment. As many contributors point out in the following chapters and as I emphasize in chapter ten, online messages are often startlingly blunt and can escalate into flaming. In the face of these uncertainties, online instructors must adopt attitudes and strategies to remind themselves and their students that they are social actors in an emotional situation. For example, one theme throughout this book is that online instructors can add typographical cues, or *emoticons*, to their messages to signal attitude and mood.

Online instructors can help develop the whole student by establishing a positive and supportive overall emotional climate through such techniques as emoticons, effective conflict management and constructive feedback (all topics that will be covered later in this book). A positive emotional climate can serve as a frame of reference for online student activities and, therefore, shapes individual expectancies, attitudes, feelings and behaviors throughout a program.

There are occasions when communication needs to be more efficient and impersonal. In those cases, one chooses to: 1) focus on the general characteristics of people, 2) ignore the issues of thinking and choice and 3) stay away from wholeness and emotions. For example, when I am talking with a bank teller, a situation where there's just the two of us in a face to face encounter (normally what one would think of as an interpersonal situation), the continuum opens up the possibility that our communication can still be on the impersonal end of the scale. Neither the bank teller nor I want to hold up a long line while we have a personal chat and recognize each other's uniqueness, feelings and choice. When two people are in a face to face situation, that does not necessarily mean that communication is or should be interpersonal. Neither interpersonal nor impersonal communication is always inappropriate. Because of expectations, time constraints, or a multitude of other factors, the impersonal approach is sometimes the only way to deal efficiently with a situation.

Online instructors must keep in mind that their situation is a different one. Two features of the online classroom combine to make it a relatively unstructured communication situation. First, it relies entirely on plain text for sending messages. Second, the plain text is temporary, appearing and disappearing from the screen. These two features make it easy for both online instructors and students to forget or ignore the person on the other end of the computer. There are no strict rules or formulas for making communication decisions in any situation, only guidelines that help people make particular choices as communicators. But it is crucially important in the online world to remember that people always have choices. They may choose to be interpersonal in such unexpected settings as teaching over a computer.

Educating the Online Student

Another of Stewart's concepts can sum up the preceding ideas—*person-building*. Person-building is the idea that the quality of each person's life is a result of the quality of the communication he or she experiences. In other words, person-building is a consequence of interpersonal communication. Communication can be a tool to accomplish certain instructional tasks, but it is also a process that affects who students are as people. As any schoolteacher knows, there is a big difference between what you say to a student (the tool part) and how you say it (the person-building part). Teachers can tell a student, "You're wrong," and emphasize being correct, or they can ask, "What's another way of getting the answer," and emphasize problem solving.

Online educators, like other educators, are fundamentally in the business of person-building. As anywhere, person-building is the foundation for learning and growth in the online classroom. It is the quality of human contact that continually develops online students—constantly reforming who they are and who they will become. Whenever the instructor communicates interpersonally online, he or she participates in the building of people and share in their learning and growth.

But other questions arise at this point: Where is this leading? What kind of people do we want our online students to become? It is important that online students are treated as unique, thinking and emotional individuals, and that we, as educators, participate in their growth. But what is the ultimate goal?

As a means for responding to these questions, I look to Virginia Voeks of San Diego University. Voeks tried a little experiment. She asked people that she knew, who have gone to college or a university, what they studied and what kinds of jobs they got. Voeks was surprised at the variety of jobs each person had held and the apparent unrelatedness of their major to their subsequent occupations. Voeks questioned whether this meant that college is unimportant? She ultimately didn't think so. To the contrary, she determined that college is even more important for it prepares students for a large range of occupations and for a widening way of living.

If online education is seen more than the electronic transmission of bits of information—if it is a human arena for interpersonal contact and person-building—then it too should be preparing students for a satisfying life. Online education is a tool to accomplish certain vocational tasks; but it is also a process that affects who students are as people. Voeks (1979) suggests some general goals that heighten the chances of a student becoming "a highly educated person" and can be readily applied to the online environment:

- *Online students need to learn various ways to understand the world and build on information.* It is important that students learn that a fund of information and ideas is a set of tools. Students will be able to solve more problems reasonably and interpret more events effectively. However, it is pointless for students to collect and store facts. The mere possession of information is worthless. Online educators can begin the journey of educating online students by recognizing that information does not constitute being "educated." That's why many online programs stress faculty members as practitioners. To be educated, online students must develop other attributes.

- *Online students should learn to see relationships and make more meaningful integrations.* "Integration" refers to the synthesis of materials and a tying together of concepts, information and ideas. With integration skills, the online student can make each new fact more meaningful and comprehensible. For example, an understanding of organizational behavior or management can be enhanced through the reading of literature. Instead of just the facts, students can confront issues about the quality of life in materials like the book *The Jungle* or the video *Wall Street.*

- *Online students should be exposed to deeper and widening interests.* The liberal arts and general studies have an important role to play in online education. They expose students to deeper interests and other ways of living. Online students should be given the chance to share in other students' lives and to gain appreciation for individual differences. College should furnish many opportunities for perceiving the value of difference and for learning to act in accord with these perceptions. For example, controversy should be encouraged in the online classroom though managed carefully. If done properly, teaching through controversy reveals a difference of opinion while promoting tolerance for diversity. Techniques like "cooperative controversy" (Bredehoft, 1991) can help the online classroom become a laboratory in which beneficial group learning takes place through controversial issues.

- When questions like, "Should new laws be enacted to limit foreign countries from buying U.S. property?" or "Are art exhibits such as photographs by Robert Mapplethorpe pornographic, and should they be supported by taxpayers' money?" are addressed through careful procedures like cooperative controversy, online students can learn new ways of thinking.

Thus, the person-building metaphor highlights the central importance of interpersonal communication and a broad education in the online environment. It suggests that online instructors can communicate in such a way as to play a role in helping students to learn information and to develop as people. Online education is not just about the transmission of information. It depends on a friendly, relaxed and congenial classroom with a teacher who shows respect for students, who is concerned about their needs and who is supportive. In other words, online education—as a process of training and developing the knowledge, skill, mind and character of learners—arises from and is sustained by broader instructional goals and practices. Although technological factors strongly influence the online learning climate, their effects must be mediated by the human interaction facilitated by the online instructor. It is the quality of relationships that is crucial. No contact is more central to the education of an online student than the human one.

Conclusion

As this chapter has attempted to outline, the way day-to-day teaching functions in the online environment is, in part, a result of how teachers perceive communication and its relationship to the human factor. Choice making is a necessary part of online communication and offers a way for responding to various instructional challenges and situations, but appropriate choices depend on the ability to see communication situations in a variety of ways. Changing the guiding metaphors used for clarifying complex communication situations helps reveal online communication choices. What might have been considered an impersonal setting is reframed to have many interpersonal possibilities. An interaction with an online student that was only seen as a phase of task completion becomes an opportunity to affect the quality of the student's life.

Overall, this chapter has attempted to reinforce the idea that effective online teaching is two-fold: the ability to transmit messages clearly and accurately, and the ability to maintain positive interpersonal relationships. In fact, the chapter has tried to tilt the balance between these two functions in the online environment a little more to the interpersonal side. In many ways, it suggests that, to paraphrase the German philosopher Karl Jaspers, the online instructor's supreme achievement in the virtual world is communication from personality to personality.

That said, I will leave you with a few reminders for improving online interpersonal communication and teaching skills:

- *Watch your communication metaphors.* Effectiveness in today's online learning environments begins with a broader, more realistic picture of the people and the communication that makes up virtual organizations.
- *Treat your online students as unique.* Use your students' names in all correspondence and have online students upload a brief autobiography at the beginning of each class. Encourage them to share their life stories as well as ideas about the course. Do not ignore the fact that even a simple thing like a message sent to a student's personal mailbox where you ask how things are going helps to build self-esteem and a positive a sense of individuality.
- *Build choice into your online courses and teaching behaviors.* People make choices about how to communicate in the online classroom based on past choices, perceptions of the current situation and the ability to see communication situations differently. Assume that you have choices when it comes to online teaching and look for possibilities. Choose to be interpersonal. Look for opportunities to treat online students as thinking human beings. Practice open communication while setting high standards.
- *Actively contribute to a positive emotional climate.* As often as possible, use interpersonal communication to encourage online interaction and to build collective trust. Manage online conflict and practice constructive feedback. In addition, as chapter three will stress, use humor. Humor is a useful online perspective, a way of looking at and coping with electronic technology and human interaction.

Finally, remember more than anything else that effective online education is more than merely sending messages or accomplishing instructional tasks—it is about building educated people.

References

Bredehoft, D.J. (1991). Cooperative controversies in the classroom. *College Teaching*, 39 (3), 122-1225.

Sproull, L. & Kiesler, S. (1991*). Connections: New Ways of Working in the Networked Organization.* Cambridge, MA: The MIT Press.

Stewart, J. (2005). *Bridges Not Walls.* New York: McGraw-Hill
    Publishing Company.

Voeks, V. (1979). *On Becoming an Educated Person.* Philadelphia:
    W.B. Saunders Company.

Weick, K. (1969). *The Social Psychology of Organizing.* Reading, MA:
    Addison-Wesley.

Chapter 2

TAMING THE LIONS AND TIGERS AND BEARS

The WRITE Way to Communicate Online

By Chad Lewis

Dorothy and her pals didn't have a choice on their journey to Oz. They had to make it to the Emerald City. Online instructors and students are in the same fix in the sense that, once committed to the virtual classroom, there's no way to avoid communicating online. And, for many, the virtual classroom holds the lions and tigers and bears of the story.

The primary purpose of this chapter is to help instructors to tame the beasts: first, by contributing to the understanding of the dynamics underlying online communication and, then, by offering perspectives, a framework and rules for improving it.

We're Not in Kansas Anymore!

Before delving into nuances of online communication, it's important to first discuss complexities of good old-fashioned, face to face communication—the sort we engage in everyday. As chapter one suggested, interpersonal communication is inherently complex. It is fraught with the potential for misunderstanding, even without the added burden of communicating through a modem.

Take, for example, the fuzzy nature of language. The words we communicate may be understandable. However, the "why" of communication may be less so. For example, you may interpret my comment that "I like fish" to mean I enjoy broiled salmon steak with lemon juice and tartar sauce when, in fact, I was really trying to communicate a special fondness for a pet goldfish named Sherbet. Words can be as slippery as gold fish.

Besides the fuzziness of language, miscommunication also occurs because of invalid *attributions*. Human beings are "sense making" creatures. We can form very clear attributions of others from just a small sample of communication and other information. We continually filter observations selectively, subject to recency and order effects, form a prototype based on those observations, and fill in the gaps of the prototype where necessary, often times erroneously (Feldman, 1981).

Here's an example. Take a second and make the choices:

Mary is healthy, wealthy and (smart, stupid).

Larry is bright, lively and (fat, slender).

Most of you decided that Mary is smart and Larry is slender. Of course, wealthy people can be stupid and bright people can be fat. However, most Americans have been socialized to make the associations of "smart" and "slender" respectively in this exercise. Of course, prototype formation concerning characteristics of Mary and Larry will become more accurate as more information about these people is, or becomes, available.

Attributions are also profoundly influenced by a person's frame of reference. Two people can receive the same communication, and as a function of coming from very different backgrounds, can reach two very different conclusions about the meaning of a particular communication.

Sometimes, the difference is simply perceptual. Independent of frame of reference, one person sees or hears something different than another, even when both parties are part of the same communication. In April 1997, a Boston DJ at WZLX-FM mentioned an incredible set of connections between the Pink Floyd album, *Dark Side of the Moon* and the film, *The Wizard of Oz*. The claim is that the album music and events on the screen coincide. (To see the magic, you have to start the album at the third roar of the MGM lion at the beginning of the film and, of course, have to watch *The Wizard of Oz* with the sound turned off.) Are the connections real? Not according to members of the band, Pink Floyd. Kennedy (1997) offers one explanation in noting: "While it is true, as anyone who's watched MTV with the sound off and radio on will confirm, that the brain is quick to transform any music into a soundtrack. Maybe this is the explanation. (p. 214)

People are constantly involved in "cognitive shorthand" associated with filling in the blanks, making assumptions based on sometimes cursory perceptual input, relying on our frame of reference as they form attributions, and striving to make sense of those around us. Although this dynamic is the basis of stereotyping, it is not necessarily bad or wrong.

14

If it were not for this cognitive shorthand, people would be extremely frustrated. It is not necessary or even valid to try to stop the process. Rather, the idea is to understand the dynamic and to reduce errors whenever possible.

The process of attribution formation I have described is inevitable and significantly influences communication whether in the home, at school or in the workplace. For example, you might communicate more warmly with a student in the future if you attribute her behavior to being unlucky, as opposed to being lazy. You might communicate more respectfully with a faculty colleague because you perceive him or her to be bright and lively, as opposed to being a "squeaky wheel." Most certainly, in The Wizard of Oz, the communication involving Dorothy and her crew was profoundly influenced by the group's collective attributions concerning the "great and powerful Oz." Witness how their perceptions and subsequent communication changed after the wizard's cover was blown.

With problems associated with fuzzy language, invalid attributions and pitfalls of using cognitive shorthand in general, it is a wonder that communication hits the mark as often as it does. To all of the challenges outlined thus far, online communication carries additional burdens. These additional "lions and tigers and bears" can quickly sink instructors who might otherwise communicate well in a traditional classroom.

A Horse of a Different Color

Online communicators are particularly prone to communicative difficulties and complexities outlined thus far because online communication excludes rich and significant cues on which people normally rely as information sources. In this regard, it is noteworthy that communication researchers have consistently found that nonverbal cues are the dominant source of meaning in interpersonal communication (Mehrabian, 1972). Yet, these cues are missing online. As a consequence, online communicators are compelled to "fill in the blanks" more frequently than they might in face to face interactions, leading to the potential for faulty prototype formation and invalid attributions discussed previously.

The added communication complexities of online can quickly lead to anxiety and hostility, feelings that might be excessive to what would normally be experienced face to face. Exchanges can quickly blow entirely out of proportion. People can come out of "left field" with surprising and often insulting language. Onliners refer to this type of communication as *flaming*. Flaming can be defined as electronic messages or retorts that express startlingly blunt, extreme and impulsive language. A flamer often says things online that he or she would never say to another person face to face.

Misunderstandings of language or faulty attributions usually lie behind every "flame." A student receives a message open to interpretation, lacks the nonverbal inputs necessary to help interpret the message appropriately, assigns faulty attributions to the message and fires back with anger and name-calling in the classroom. I will talk about solutions to this particular dilemma shortly.

Here are a few other differences between online and face- to-face communication of which you should be aware:

- *Individuals in computer-mediated groups are relatively more uninhibited.* Flaming is only one outcome of this dynamic. Online group members are also more willing to disclose personally sensitive information relative to face to face interaction (Siegel, Dubrovsky, Kiesler & McGuire, 1986). The intimacy that can spring up within the virtual classroom is amazing. Students often comment that they quickly come to know their virtual classmates much better than co-workers and neighbors, even when the latter relationships have been of long duration.
- *Status differences play less of a role in an online environment.* The fact that a person is "The Instructor" or "The Boss" or "Knows What They Are Talking About" has less of an inhibiting effect on interactions (Sproull & Kiesler, 1992; Harasim, 1988). Some of the most successful online programs in the United States are adult centered and emphasize a facilitative, rather than a professorial, approach in the classroom. Instructors who are accustomed to the traditional lecture method and a "professor as God" dynamic will be surprised by the cheekiness of online students.
- *Interaction in online groups tends to be more evenly distributed among group members* (Kiesler, 1984). This aspect of online education is a huge advantage. I have often had students comment that they engage in online classroom discussion to a much greater degree than when in a traditional classroom. "Squeaky wheels" get shut down online because everyone has equal access to the instructor and to interaction in the virtual classroom.
- *Online consensus decision making takes significantly longer than when group members interact face to face (Kiesler, 1984).* It tends to be more difficult for online groups to reach agreement. This dynamic significantly affects group projects. It can be tough for groups of more than three students to efficiently complete their work. Quite often, they must resort to conference calls on the phone. For this reason, when

assigning membership for student projects, I like to assign students to work in dyads.

The balance of this chapter provides information useful for constructively dealing with the dynamics of online communication described to this point.

The WRITE Way to Communicate Online

Acronyms are helpful for remembering useful concepts. I like to use an acronym, based on a bad pun that is helpful whenever I engage in online interaction: the WRITE Way to communicate online. The WRITE Way involves communicating online in a manner that is (W)arm, (R)esponsive, (I)nquisitive, (T)entative and (E)mpathetic. Here's an explanation of each component:

(W)armth

Words on a screen are two-dimensional. Reading these words in isolation of nonverbal communication cues lends itself to "coolness" that can lead to overreaction and flaming. In this regard, online communicators sometimes lose perspective—acting as though messages are going into the relative privacy of a text file saved to the user's hard drive, rather than being downloaded and read by perhaps hundreds, even thousands, of people. People, in turn, read two-dimensional words in isolation, misinterpret fuzzy language or experience faulty attributions and react. Pretty soon it's—BOOM!—flaming communication that leads to embarrassment, chagrin, guilt, shame and anger. In short, it is a whole plethora of potentially counterproductive human emotions.

Increasing warmth online does not have to be "touchy feely"—giving people the electronic equivalent of sloppy hugs and kisses. Rather, increasing warmth means to decrease the psychic distance among communicators. Being warm online is a way of reminding others (and you) that it's people who are engaged in communication, not software. There are several effective ways in which to improve online warmth.

1. *Use the telephone when necessary.* Phoning a student to clarify a point or to negotiate a particularly sensitive issue should occur when email just does not cut it. Some onliners think electronic messages should suffice for all communication. I do not agree. An occasional phone call can be useful. Its efficacy can be seen in a common revelation that occurs when two onliners speak together for the first time. Invariably, when I phone my students, the

first thing we discuss on the phone is the fact that "real people" are behind the words on the screen.

2. *Send sensitive information to private mailboxes.* It is usually much more helpful to offer "constructive feedback" privately. This approach is akin to offering feedback behind closed doors.

3. *Incorporate warmth into written text.* Professional writers are able to convey a wide range of emotions. It is much tougher for normal mortals to do this. I have found it helpful to occasionally write about my family and interests. Sometimes, I will tell a joke, though the joke needs to be a "sure thing" because humor can easily backfire online. Example of a "sure thing" joke: Q: What has two knees and swims? A: A two-knee (tuna) fish. (Sorry for that...the opportunity was there and I just couldn't help myself.) Interesting examples and metaphors also sometimes work well. For example, I have had a lot of fun trying to relate this chapter to examples from *The Wizard of Oz*. Hopefully, my struggle to find connections has also been interesting to the reader.

4. *Describe the setting from which you are writing, the weather or music to which you're listening.* Online warmth of this kind helps students to place you in a human setting.

5. *Play with language.* This suggestion adds warmth and contributes to understanding as long as it's not overdone. One way to have fun with language and symbols online is to use an occasional *emoticon*. Emoticons represent a way of bringing so-called nonverbal cues into online communication though, technically, emoticons are not "nonverbal" communication because they are intentional and symbolic.

My favorite emoticons are the smiley and winky: :-) ;-). The former emoticon conveys intended humor; the latter that the writer is poking fun in a non-threatening way. An occasional frown :-(is okay as long as the receiver of a message understands the dissatisfaction isn't being directed at him or her. But use emoticons only as an occasional seasoning. A steady diet gets irritating, as well as confusing.

(R)esponsiveness

Online communication is usually asynchronous. This means people can wait several days before getting a response to a message. The waiting period can feed into invalid attributions, many of which are negative ("Chad hasn't replied to my message! Hmmm.... guess he doesn't really think much of my ideas").

A solution is to set deadlines, or otherwise be consistent, in terms of when you give feedback. This reduces anxiety and creates an expectation on the part of students of when they should hear back from you. Once this expectation is satisfied through timely provision of feedback, trust—a positive contributor to warmth—will be reinforced. Try to return personal messages as soon as possible and set up a regular rhythm of communication for other responses. Interestingly, instructors who upload feedback to students on a regular schedule—for example, by noon every Saturday—tend to get better student evaluations than do those that get feedback to students more quickly, but who are also inconsistent, getting papers back the next day, one week, three days later and so forth.

Another aspect of responsiveness is *redundancy*. Remember to provide occasional reminders to students. Think of issuing reminders as a proactive type of responsiveness. An interesting aspect of online communication is that it's possible to have a perfect memory of what "was said." Unfortunately, it can also be difficult for students to "remember" what is said when it's buried in thousands of gigabytes of information that have blasted through the class. Consequently, don't be surprised if students fail to act on an online request or forget, particularly if information is part of a larger message, or part of a succession of messages on related topics. The use of short messages and redundancy helps to allay this problem and keeps online communicators on track.

(I)nquisitiveness

Defensiveness is reduced if people ask questions rather than make statements. It is usually more constructive to ask a person *why* than it is to tell them *what*. Inquisitiveness serves two important purposes: Besides reducing defensiveness, it often provides information that is useful for solving a problem, resolving an issue or whatever. Bringing valid information to bear on online communicative exchanges is almost always a good idea.

Glinda the Good Witch's attribution that Dorothy was a witch missed the mark, but her timely question "Are you a good witch, or a bad witch?" secured information that saved the day. What would have happened if Glinda and the Munchkins had assumed Dorothy to be a bad witch and had attacked her? She never would have learned about the Wizard of Oz, the Yellow Brick Road, or discovered the Scarecrow, then Tin Man and Cowardly Lion.

(T)entativeness

Defensiveness is reduced when people hear or read, "It appears that..." as opposed to, "It is..." Inquisitiveness and tentativeness work well together. A question—framed in a tentative manner—reduces defensiveness and can also contribute valuable information (e.g. "Don't you think it'd be better if we...).

Use tentative language and posturing with students, unless the situation dictates otherwise. The concept of sending "I" rather than "you" messages works as well in online writing as it does in oral interaction. It's often better to say or to write, "I believe..." rather than to say or write "you are...."

Sometimes, instructors must make absolute statements. You must occasionally send "you" messages. Communication with students and others might otherwise degenerate into a sloppy, gooey, indeterminate mess not unlike conversations that occur when a bunch of counselors get together to talk out a problem. :-) When to be absolute and when to be tentative is up to you. It is a judgment call.

(E)mpathy

An important aspect of online communication is to put yourself in the shoes of your audience. Always consider the position of your students. There are a wide variety of issues to keep in mind. For example, a student can be a highly effective, intelligent contributor in the virtual classroom even if he or she misspells words or uses poor grammar. What if this student speaks and writes English as a second language? I tend to cut such students some slack in informal classroom discussion, though formal assignments must still be of a high caliber.

Sometimes students send email excuses for tardy work or offer all types of interesting reasons for failure to perform. Some of this communication should be taken with a grain of salt. However, I don't have a problem with working with students who experience occasional difficulty associated with their schedules. I figure students choose to attend online for good reasons that often pertain to hectic lives. It would be contradictory, besides not being empathetic, to put the hammer down on these students without some consideration.

Empathy also involves inquisitiveness. An idea I have always found to be helpful is to be inquisitive if you need information to better understand your audience. Ask a lot of questions if necessary. Gathering valid information helps to reduce the likelihood of invalid attributions and prototype formation in online communication.

To summarize this section, The WRITE Way to online communication involves communicating in a manner that is (W)arm, (R)esponsive, (I)nquisitive, (T)entative and (E)mpathetic:

- (W)armth means to use the telephone when necessary; send sensitive information to private mailboxes and incorporate warmth into text.
- (R)esponsiveness means to set deadlines, or otherwise be consistent, in terms of when you give feedback and to provide occasional reminders.
- (I)nquisitiveness means to ask questions. This allays defensiveness on the part of others and collects information that might improve attributions and understanding.
- (T)entativeness means to use tentative language and posturing, unless the situation dictates otherwise.
- (E)mpathy means to put yourself in the shoes of your students and to perhaps cut them some slack from time-to-time.

Follow the Yellow Brick Road!

Proper form—following the rules—is important in most human undertakings. Among a gazillion examples of this are good table manners, proper greetings and the effort taken by Dorothy and her troop to properly prepare for meeting the great Wizard of Oz. Online communication has its own protocol. Some learn it the hard way, by being flamed in a public forum when they goof. Even long-time onliners occasionally slip up and get roasted. In the interest of helping you to avoid this unpleasant experience, I conclude this chapter with advice based on a 1994 post concerning "netiquette" from *Time* magazine's web site. All of these kernels of wisdom work well in the classroom, as well as in general online communication:

- *Keep your posts brief and to the point.* A variation on this piece of advice is to use short paragraphs. Not sure where I learned this tidbit, but a lot of short paragraphs are decidedly easier to follow on a computer monitor than is one "screen buster."
- *Encourage students to stick to the subject of a particular thread or classroom discussion.* Occasionally, you'll run into a classroom full of exuberant students who genuinely like one another and want to talk about everything. You may want to consider setting up another electronic meeting as an outlet for classes that are particularly chatty.

If your conferencing software precludes this option, then you may have to play traffic cop to keep discussion focused on course material.

- *If you are responding to a message, quote the relevant passages or summarize it for those who may have missed it. Don't copy in the entire message to which you're replying unless it's short.* Conferencing software tends to paste in the entire message to which participants are responding. This means that users have to consciously go in and remove irrelevant portions. It is important to remind students to do this. Otherwise, too many unnecessary kilobytes end up in the virtual classroom.

- *Never publish private email without permission.* I occasionally respond in the virtual classroom to a private student query. However, I do this only if a student's question is innocuous and when my response needs to be read by the student's classmates. Sometimes, students need to be encouraged to direct their questions to the classroom, rather than to the instructor's private email address. Obviously, truly private messages need to be kept private.

- *Discourage students from posting test messages or cluttering up the virtual classroom with "I agree" and "Me too!" messages.* Participation can be an important component of an online class. To the extent that this is true, the question of how to define participation invariably pops up. Students need to be encouraged to upload substantive replies to course-related messages. I address the "me too" and "I agree" approach to participation by discussing this problem in my course syllabus. I also gently address this issue in private student feedback to the extent it has occurred during the week.

- *Don't type in all caps.* (IT'S RUDE AND IS LIKE SHOUTING!) I have one exception to this rule: I employ caps when grading student papers. Red pencils don't work in a word processor, but upper case works great. The use of upper case and asterisks helps to **SEPARATE** instructor comments from the text of student papers.

A Concluding Thought

It would be great if we could simply tap ruby heels and instantly be whisked off to the Kansas of effective online communication. The reality is we must start over with each new student group; and the communication dynamics discussed in this chapter are relentless and relatively unforgiving.

I have not found any shortcuts, with the possible exception of phoning each student early on. Such communication provides students with the information helpful for improving attributions of their instructor, though it doesn't help with attributions of classmates. If you have the time and other resources, calling each of your students might be a good idea. Doing so is still a relatively clunky "solution," however.

Someday, technology may improve to the point where we can take off the straitjacket of the WRITE Way and other comparable, disciplined approaches to online communication. Until then, we must compensate.

References

Feldman, J.M. (1981). Beyond attribution theory: cognitive processes in performance appraisal. *Journal of Applied Psychology*, 66, 127-148.

Harasim, L.M. (1988). *Online group learning/teaching methods (technical paper #7).* Education Evaluation Centre, the Ontario Institute for Studies in Education.

Kennedy, H. (1997). Rainbow in the dark. *Guitar World*, 17, 214.

Kiesler, S. (1984). Social psychological aspects of computer-mediated communication. *American Psychologist*, 39, 1123-1134.

Mehrabian, A. (1972). Tactics of Social Influence. Englewood Cliffs, NJ: Prentice-Hall.

Siegel, J; Dubrovsky, V.; Kiesler, S.; & McGuire, T. (1986). Group processes in computer-mediated communication. *Organizational Behavior and Human Decision Processes,* 37, 157- 187.

Sproull, L. & Kiesler, S. (1992). *Connections.* Cambridge, MA: The MIT Press.

About the Author

Chad received his M.Ed. from Western Washington University. He teaches at the University of Phoenix Online and at Everett Community College, and can be contacted at ctlewis@everettcc.edu.

Chapter 3

TALKING THE TALK

Humor & Other Forms of Online Communication

By Arlene Hiss

The purpose of this chapter is to discuss how online facilitators should "talk" to their students. As chapters one and two emphasized, carefully chosen words and expressions help make online teaching a positive experience. In this chapter, I want to look at specific forms of online "teacher talk," conventionalized ways of communicating and writing in the online instructor role.

Teaching online is unlike any other educational experience. Faculty and students have to rely solely on the written word. There is no body language or eye contact to depend upon as in the onsite classroom. Teaching online is quite unique. Because typical online instructors deal mainly with the written word, it is not always possible to determine race, ethnicity, physical characteristics, physical challenges, or in some cases, even gender. For example, I mistakenly thought a student was a man based on the written communication in the classroom. There were no clues such as this person claiming to have a wife or husband. Four weeks into the class, I discovered he was a she.

A variety of components to "teacher talk" will be discussed in this chapter: *control talk, humor, special language* and an *"andragogical"* approach (Knowles, 1978). The facilitator who fails to pay special attention to these areas will run into difficulty.

(Editor's Note: It should be mentioned here that rather than refer to descriptors such as *teacher* and *professor*, the author uses the label *facilitator*. This is not to demote the concept of being a teacher. There is already too much of that in the online world where professional teachers are handed a course curriculum and directed to teach it as it is. Teachers are more than facilitators. Their creative power lies in creating unique instructional methods for satisfying course objectives and they should be allowed to do their job. But effective online instruction is also *facilitative* and effective online instructors guide classroom discourse with only a minimum of traditional lecturing.)

Control Talk

Usually, the idea of controlling a process has a negative, even dictatorial connotation. That is not the way it is meant here. *Control talk* refers to any communication used by an online facilitator to set tone, to clarify expectations and to convey meaning that is understood by all. I will begin with a discussion of *tone*.

Communicating online can be sterile, which, in turn, can intimidate new students. Such students have never experienced the virtual classroom; they often need a lot of handholding. The first experience a new online student has often determines his or her likelihood for future success. Consequently, the first facilitator that students encounter in entry courses must have a good working knowledge of the conferencing software in order to help new students find their way. They must be extremely responsive to the student's problems and needs. The facilitator needs to have a caring persona rather than one that is cold and aloof. Messages sent by facilitators should come across naturally, as though they were speaking to students face to face. Students, in turn, will tend to model the facilitator's communication style, contributing to a warmer classroom environment.

An online facilitator should never be sarcastic. Sarcasm opens up a plethora of problems as students follow suit. Also, it is important to re-read your messages to soften any questionable statements. Overall, in terms of establishing a supportive classroom tone, a good motto to live by is: When in doubt – don't.

As chapter two observed, sometimes a "flame war" occurs. Flaming involves online conflict that erupts into personal or rude attacks. A facilitator who leads emotionally charged classes—such as, say, a course dealing with managerial ethics— might experience flame wars more often. There is a multitude of viewpoints whenever one deals with personal morals, personal values and personal ethics in the classroom, many of which are potentially upsetting.

Though skillful online facilitators carefully craft responses to help extinguish flames; ideally, they set a tone that avoids the likelihood of conflict. Prevention is the key. Some students are strong-willed and unbending in the virtual classroom. Effective "control talk" by the facilitator helps to chill out such students before they build up a head of steam. In this regard, a private email or phone call to a particularly volatile student can also be a good idea.

Facilitators should not become irate or "lose their cool" when dealing with flames. In some cases, the flame war can be diffused with humor. If an entire class is involved in conflict, a note to the whole class is in order. It is important not to overreact to flaming, an approach that can easily create even more negative reactions from the students. By using calming language and by not dwelling on negatives, the students will usually move on. Do not ignore flames; but do not overreact.

Much of the time, a facilitator does not need to say or do anything when flames engulf the online classroom because students constructively handle the situation on their own. Such a happenstance can be a great learning experience, one that prepares students to better work within teams in the real world.

In short, the way the online facilitator communicates to the class sets the tone—how the facilitator goes, so goes the class. Students cue off of the facilitator. A sarcastic or rude facilitator might very well produce a sarcastic and rude online class. In addition, a facilitator who is not very "visible" will likely have students who are also invisible. (Facilitators should post notes regularly to class; their name should appear frequently.) And if a facilitator uses humor, students will also feel comfortable expressing humor. (More about online humor will be discussed later.)

Interestingly, effective online control talk can be indirect; it is often subtle. A carefully timed question to the classroom might help restore order. If online students are chatting excessively, a facilitator might set up a separate chat meeting or opportunity. In this instance, one of two things happens. Either students constrain chit-chat within an appropriate venue, or they take the hint and cut down on chatter. Either way, it is win-win situation.

Effective "control talk" and other facilitating behaviors online help to set a productive tone in the classroom. It also helps facilitators to clarify expectations and to create a structure that contributes to learning. Here are some tips that relate to online expectations and structure:

Top Ten Hints for Success

1. Encourage online students to contact the technical help desk if they run into technical difficulties. The sooner technical problems are solved, the better.
2. Remember the 4-F motto. Be: *Firm, Fair, Flexible and Fun!*

3. Reply to student autobiographies with a personal note about something the student said. Online students love to be warmly welcomed. Talk about their dogs, kids, hobbies or anything non-work or school-related.

4. Have your syllabus ready to go at the beginning of an online course and have it clearly state when all assignments are due and the points or percentage of the grade for each assignment.

5. Always have class materials (e.g. lectures) uploaded the day prior to the first day of the classroom week, or whenever you previously said materials would be uploaded. Be consistent!

6. Always get back to questions from your online students as soon as possible, but no later than 24 hours.

7. Never leave your online class for an extended time without telling students when you will be back. If, for some reason, you cannot get through online (computer crash etc.), contact your school immediately so that your class can be informed immediately of the problem.

8. Try to send students a handout, message, thought for the day or *something* every day. Online students need to know you are there. One idea: shorten up longer uploads into handouts that can be submitted periodically during the week.

9. Give feedback and grades on a regular schedule every week. Online students hate not knowing how they are doing. Send grades and feedback frequently and periodically, on a regular schedule. Always provide some positives in your feedback.

10. *Maintain your sense of humor!*

Humor in the Online Classroom

A student of mine once said, "Humor belongs.... it enhances any experience including learning when the brain dumps 'crazy chemicals' into the body." When people are laughing, their brains seem to operate more efficiently and symmetrically. Laughter equals relaxation. A person cannot simultaneously laugh and be tense.

Humor in the workplace has recently become an important topic in management publications such as the *Harvard Business Review, Wall Street Journal, Training Magazine* and *Business Week*. Management consulting firm Robert half International reported that in a study of personnel directors at 100 of the nation's largest corporations (Roueche, 1996), 84 percent report that people with a sense of humor are more creative, less rigid and more willing to try new ideas and methods. Hodge-Cronin and Associates, a management consulting firm in Rosemont, Illinois, regularly conducts surveys on humor in the workplace. In their 1994 study, *Humor in the Workplace,* they surveyed approximately 600 top executives from various-sized companies and found:

- One hundred percent of the executives responding stated that humor has a positive impact in a business situation.
- Ninety-five percent of the executives stated that all things being equal, they would more likely hire a candidate with a sense of humor.
- Eighty percent of the executives stated that humor can have a positive effect when dealing with foreign executives provided you understand the culture and use the humor appropriately.
- Forth-three percent believed that the use of humor is decreasing while the demand is increasing.

One of humor's most widely promoted benefits is that humor appears to fulfill an individual's need to be part of a group, an important consideration in the technologically dependent and *deindividuated* environment of online learning.

In addition, humor promotes novelty, divergent thinking, creative problem solving and risk taking. The *incongruity theory of humor* helps explain how an individual is able to find an unexpected or novel way to approach a problem using a sense of humor. When something is incongruous, it does not fit a person's conceptual patterns and ordinary ways of looking at things. Humor gives people a way to gain distance from the incongruity and to benefit creatively from the new ideas. *In other words, as online instructors, you can help your students learn and help prepare them for the workplace by using humor in your classes.*

Obviously, there are many benefits to using humor in the online classroom. Humor warms up what might otherwise be a cold and sterile environment. Students need to feel comfortable with their classmates, facilitator and the environment so that a positive learning experience can occur. According to Hill (1988), laughter in the classroom is a sign that students are enjoying the learning process rather than viewing it as dull and boring. A smile can come right through the computer monitor via your words. A smile shows openness and enthusiasm. Appropriate humor generally brings the facilitator and students together. I personally like the motto: Laugh and learn.

Humor also eases stress for the online student. New students are typically nervous and highly stressed when they first enter the virtual classroom. Once students are made comfortable, perhaps by laughing at a funny anecdote or topic-related humorous story, their anxiety lessens.

Humor should never be a substitute for substance, but rather should serve as a "seasoning" that enhances the online learning process. A lecture that is sprinkled with topic-related funny stories will be remembered for a long time to come. Look for amusing anecdotes that can be used to illustrate difficult concepts and for analogies that transform abstract ideas into more familiar examples. Students comprehend material better when it is related to a funny story (Hill, 1988). I ask new students to relate a positive and a negative learning experience in their past. Nearly half of them list a facilitator's sense of humor as a positive. Student end-of-course surveys also reflect the positives associated with a facilitator's sense of humor.

The following story is an example of humor that might happen in an online logic class and serves the purpose of establishing a more informal tone:

The professor writes to his online class on logic.

"By way of introduction," the professor began, "let me begin the course by posing a question. Suppose two men were digging a well. Upon completion, they come out of the hole and one is clean while the other one is dirty. Which man will go and take the shower?"

Several students responded:

"The dirty one, of course," one student typed.

"Really," wrote the professor. "Remember, they can only see each other, not themselves,"

"I see, now," responded another student. "The clean one sees the dirty one, assumes that he is dirty, too, and takes the shower."

"I see we have a lot of work ahead of us," types the professor. "How could two men be digging a well and one of them not get dirty?"

A group that laughs together stays together. An online class that can have fun together will be more cohesive and, in turn, inclined to be more productive. A group that laughs together shares a common experience. Laughing is like yawning, it is contagious (Hill, 1988). Here are a few other suggestions:

- *One-liners are great for loosening up an online class.* Think funny! Online gives the advantage of the time to think of a snappy "comeback." An online student might kiddingly ask me to "forget about assigning a final paper." My comment back might be "In your dreams, bucko!" Another example might be, rather than make a boring statement such as "You bet" or "That is true" to a student comment, I might say, "You can bet your cowboy boots on it." Small and seemingly insignificant tweaks can change a boring statement into a humorous one while still saying the same thing. My favorite is when a student will share that one of the reasons they like online so much is because she can go to school in her pajamas. My response to that is, "You wear that much?" I like to tell the students that this is the only "clothing optional" university around and we don't have to worry about makeup or bad hair days.
- *Self-effacing humor can work well.* When online facilitators laugh at their own mistakes, rather than cover up or make excuses, this sends the message to students that the facilitator is human and that it's okay to make mistakes once in awhile. Hopefully, students will feel comfortable about laughing at, and learning from, their own mistakes.
- *Have a folder of funny stories that relates to a particular topic under discussion.* Here are a couple of my favorites that I use when discussing resistance to change:

> **Humor has a very significant role in defusing resistance to change. There will always be somebody who sees the negative side of change, such as the old farmer getting a look at his first car. He watched as the proud new owner cranked and toiled to no avail. The old farmer kept repeating to all that would listen, "It ain't gonna start." Once it started and the driver jumped behind the wheel, his message changed: "You ain't gonna be able to stop the thing!"**

> **An efficiency expert was hired to go through a company and make recommendations for changes. He went into the**

plant and to the first worker he saw standing by a lathe, he said, "What is your job around here?" The worker said, "To be honest about it, I have nothing to do." From the plant, the efficiency expert went upstairs to the office staff, spotted a woman sitting behind a typewriter and asked, "What is your job around here? What do you do?" She said, "To be frank about it, I really don't have anything to do." "Ah hah!" He replied, "Duplication!"

Online humor can be effective when used well, but is also risky. People love to laugh and, if you can make them laugh, they will generally listen to what you have to say. However, if you, as an online facilitator, are uncomfortable with using humor, you should not force it. And, needless to say, but I will say it anyway, humor should *always* be G-rated. Any facilitator should stay completely away from any racial, ethnic, gender-related, political, religious or alternative lifestyle humor.

Not all humor works, so a few words of caution are in order. It is a mistake to confuse professionalism with seriousness. You should take your education and teaching seriously, but take yourself lightly in your online classes. On the other hand, do not make your classes a comedy club. Misplaced humor can be destructive and distracting from the topic at hand. The best philosophy is to laugh hard and to work hard.

Online students need to realize that a sense of humor is a skill that they can and should develop to enhance their learning and their opportunities in the workplace. But sometimes humor can detract from a serious message or discussion. It is important to find a balance. It is up to the facilitator to set boundaries when using humor and to insure that humor is limited and appropriate. It is easy to be misunderstood online. What you intend to be humorous, another party might see as offensive. Consequently, use *emoticons* to convey meaning—for instance, if you send a message intended to be funny, be sure to include a smiley :-). Tease gently with a winkey ;-). Many facilitators resist use of emoticons, (they are not true nonverbals) but their use can spell the difference between constructive humor and destructive misunderstanding. The next section continues with further discussion of emoticons and their use.

Special Languages

When onsite facilitators are face to face with students, they can use nonverbal expressions to communicate in conjunction with words. Online communicators, however, usually depend mostly on words. Therefore, it is relatively more challenging to strive for clarity. The facilitator cannot afford to be as vague or ambiguous as in an onsite classroom. I try to communicate online just as I would if a person was facing me, plus I might add in a few emoticons to clarify my meaning. Emoticons come from several sources. It is not necessary to use even a fraction of them. In fact, I mostly use the "smiley" and the "winkey." Here are a few of the more creative ones:

HAPPY, SMILING, LAUGHING

:-)	smiling; agreeing
:-D	laughing
|-)	hee hee
|-D	ho ho
:->	hey hey
;-)	so happy, I'm crying
:'-)	crying with joy
\~/	full glass; my glass is full

TEASING, MISCHIEVOUS

;-)	winking; just kidding
'-)	winking; just kidding
;->	devilish wink
:*)	clowning
:-T	keeping a straight face

AFFIRMING, SUPPORTING

:^D	"Great! I like it!"
8-]	"Wow, maaan"
:-o	"Wow!"
^5	high five
^	thumbs up
(::()::)	band aid; offering help or support

UNHAPPY, SAD

:-(	frowning; boo hoo
:(	sad
:-<	really sad
:-c	really unhappy

:-C	really bummed
&-|	tearful
:'	crying
:'-(	crying and really sad
:-|	grim
:[	really down
:-[	pouting
_/	"my glass is empty"

ANGRY, SARCASTIC

>:-<	angry
:-||	angry
:-@	screaming
:-V	shouting
:-r	sticking tongue out
>:-<	absolutely livid!!
:-,	smirk
:-P	nyahhhh!
:->	bitingly sarcastic

SURPRISED, INCREDULOUS, SKEPTICAL

:>	What?
:@	What?
:Q	What?
:-o	"uhh oh!" OR surprise
;-)	sardonic incredulity
:O	shocked
8-|	eyes wide with surprise
:-/	skeptical
8-O	"Omigod!!"
:-C	just totally unbelieving
|-{	"Good Grief!" (Charlie Brown)

From time-to-time, online communicators may use abbreviations as a "special language" to convey meaning, like kids do when they "text:" Known as chatspeak, txt, txtspk, texting language or txt talk, here's a good list of them, but you will have to look up the risky ones yourself:

AFAIK	As Far As I Know
AFK	Away from keyboard
Alwz	Always
ASAP	As soon as possible
ATB	All the best
ATK	At the keyboard
ATM	At the moment
A3	Anytime, Anywhere, Anyplace
B	Be
B4	Before
B4N	Bye for now
BCNU	Be seeing you
BAK	Back at keyboard
BBL	Be back later
BBS	Be back soon
BFN/B4N	Bye for now
BOL	Best of luck
BRB	Be right back
BRT	Be right there
BTW	By the way
C	See
CU	See you
CUB L8R	Call you back later
CU@	See you at
CUL	See you later
CYA	See you around, See ya
CMi	Call me
CMON	Come On
CUB L8R	Call you back later
Dk	Don't know
DNR	Dinner
doN	Doing
Dur?	Do you remember

E2eg	Ear to ear grin
EOD	End of discussion
EOL	End of lecture
EVRY1	Everyone
EZ	Easy

FAQ	Frequently asked questions
FC	Fingers crossed
F2F	Face to face
F2T	Free to talk
FITB	Fill in the blank
FOMCL	Fell out of my chair laughing
FYEO	For your eyes only
FYA	For your amusement
FYI	For your information
F2F	Face to face
F2T	Free to talk

GAL	Get a life
GMTA	Great minds think alike
GR8	Great!
GTSY	Glad to see you
GUDLUK	Good luck
G9	Genius

h2cus	Hope to see you soon
H8	Hate
HAGN	Have a good night
HAND	Have a nice day
HRU	How are you
HTH	Hope that helps

IAC	In any case
IC	I See
IDK	I don't know
IIRC	If I recall correctly
IMO	In my opinion
IMHO	In my honest (or humble) opinion
IMI	I mean it

IMTNG	I am in a meeting
IOW	In other words
IUSS	If you say so
J4F	Just for fun
JK	Just kidding
JstCllMe	Just call me
KHUF	Know how you feel
KISS	Keep it simple, Stupid
KIT	Keep in touch
LOL	Laughing out loud
LTNS	Long time no see
LtsGt2gthr	Lets get together
lyN	Lying
L8	Late
L8r	Later
MTE	My thoughts exactly
MYOB	Mind your own business
NRN	No reply necessary
NA	No access
NC	No comment
NE1	Anyone
NITING	Anything
No1	No one
NP	No problem
nufN	Nothing
NWO	No way out
OIC	Oh, I see
OTOH	On the other hand
O4U	Only for you

PCME	Please call me
pl&	Planned
PLS	Please
po$bl	Possible
PTB	Please Text Back
PUKS	Pick Up Kids
QPSA?	Que pasa? (what's happening?)
R	Are
RGDS	Regards
RINGL8	Running Late
RLR	Earlier
ROFL	Rolling on the floor laughing
ROTG	Rolling on the ground
RU?	Are you?
RUOK	Are You OK?
SETE	Smiling ear to ear
SOL	Sooner or later
SME1	Someone
SPK	Speak
SPK 2 U L8R	Speak to you later
SRY	Sorry
SWG	Scientific wild guess
T+	Think positive
Thx	Thanks
TIC	Tongue in Cheek
T2Go	Time to go
T2ul	Talk to you later
U	You
U2	You too
UR	You are
VRI	Very

W@	What
W8N	Waiting
WAN2	Want to
WB	Welcome Back
WRT	With respect to
WRU	Where are you?
WTF	What the heck?
WTG	Way To Go!
WTMPI	Way Too Much Personal Information
W8	Wait
W84M	Wait for me
XLNT	Excellent
Y	Why?
YR	Your
ZZZZZ	Sleeping

Another effective online technique involves communicating naturally in a conversational (as opposed to academic) tone. From an online perspective, this is "special language" because in a very technically dependent learning environment, there is a special need to avoid academic jargon that sometimes finds its way into a traditional classroom. If facilitators type as they talk, their communication will come across as being warm and friendly. (I have tried to use this approach in writing this chapter).

Finally, the online medium has developed special labels that also constitute a "special language." Lectures are often called any number of names online. The most common one is *lecturette*. There are many facilitators, however, that do not care for either the term *lecture* or *lecturette*. They coin new names such as "Thoughts from Toni," or "Hiss-A-Grams," or "Shuey's Shoebox." This gives a less formal feel to what is actually a lecture and contributes to online facilitation as I defined it earlier in this chapter.

An interesting term online communicators sometimes use is *lurking*. As ominous as it may sound, lurking merely means someone is observing a class but is not participating. *Lurkers* are hidden from sight. For this reason, from an ethical standpoint, it is vitally important to announce any lurkers to your classes.

Here are some other terms that are technical in nature and specific to online classes. Several of these terms relate to virtual academic programs that use particular software as a conferencing system. Nevertheless, the principle underlying the term can still be applied to other platforms. Rather than list these terms alphabetically, I have listed them by relationship:

Meeting Room or Forum: A "bulletin board" meeting room or forum open to those who have been invited.

Branch or Thread: A meeting room that has been branched from a main meeting room. All people who are in the "meeting room" are able to join the "branch" or often create such a thread on their own.

Read-Only Meeting or Forum: A meeting created to be "read-only," so that only the creator can write to that room. Such a forum might work well as a "lecture hall."

Attachment: By doing this, all formatting remains intact; longer notes can be sent; graphics, charts, photos, spreadsheets and PowerPoint slides can also be sent this way.

Notes/Messages/Posts: These are notes that users send to one another and to meeting rooms.

Reply: This is when a person wants to send a return note or respond to a message that has been received.

Logon: Connecting online.

Upload: Send mail out.

Download: Receive mail in.

Onsite: Classes that are held in real time in a physical classroom.

An "Andragogical" Approach

In recent years, some educators have begun to distinguish between *pedagogy* that relates to traditional education and *andragogy* that is adult centered. Even if an online classroom is populated with teenagers, the virtual medium requires student discipline that presumes a high level of maturity and a facilitator approach that presumes he or she is leading adults.

One of the biggest mistakes an online facilitator can make is to treat the students as children. A facilitator who "talks down" to students or patronizes them can expect problems. Another area that spells trouble for facilitators is to communicate as though they are the only experts in class.

An adult-centered perspective assumes that students can bring a wealth of information and experience to a class. In many cases, adult online students may be as knowledgeable as a facilitator in a particular area. The facilitator should make such students feel comfortable about sharing their expertise without the threat of being reprimanded or ridiculed. Besides using humor, a facilitator can ask questions that draw on student experiences and knowledge, and then the facilitator can bounce off student responses by contributing other information and insight. I have found that when an online facilitator says too much or otherwise dominates discussion, adult learners have a tendency to clam up. They are inclined to not want to disagree with the "expert."

Another way to utilize the expertise of adult learners is to create assignments that ask students to teach other students around a topic with which they have knowledge. Online students are able to discuss, debate, learn from each other and take away new ideas that did not come exclusively from the facilitator.

Conclusion

Teaching online can be a wonderful and rewarding experience to the extent that (1) facilitators are warm and caring and not afraid to have a sense of humor; (2) they carefully choose words in order to constructively control classroom processes related to the environment, dialogue and tone; and (3) they talk *to* students and not *at* them. There is special language to learn and to use, and the need to presume a high level of self-discipline and maturity on the part of students.

Learning to use these elements of online "teacher talk" is like learning to ride a bicycle. Once a facilitator successfully captures the parameters of teacher talk in day-to-day facilitating, its nuances remain and will hold across a wide variety of online instructional challenges. I hope my observations help you to get in the virtual saddle and to have a smooth and enjoyable ride. CUL ;->

References

Hill, D.J. (1988). *Humor in the classroom.* Springfield, Ill: Charles C Thomas Publisher.

Rouche, S.D. (Ed.) (1996). Humor's role in preparing future leaders. *Innovation Abstracts*, 19, 20.

About the Author

Arlene received her Ph.D. in leadership and human behavior from United States International University. Arlene has taught online for the University of Phoenix, Capella University, Jones International University and Upper Iowa University where she trains online faculty. She can be contacted at Arlene_Hiss@uiuonline.org.

Chapter 4

THE ELEMENTS OF EFFECTIVE
ONLINE TEACHING

Overcoming the Barriers to Success

by Anita Bischoff

Students often choose a group-based online learning environment because they enjoy learning from other working adults. Their interest in learning is maintained when the instructor and other students share in their journey towards greater understanding of course topics.

Online students learn not only from their instructors, who provide content expertise and feedback to each individual, but also from other adult learners in the classroom. Instructors expertly facilitate discussions that help working adults to apply the lessons from their texts and the instructors' lectures to their work lives. Consequently, online instruction can be every bit as effective as a regular classroom in serving working adult students (Kauffman, 1996).

The key to online education's effectiveness lies in large part with the facilitator. As past Director of Academic Affairs at the University of Phoenix Online, I identified certain competencies that directly enhance teaching and learning in a discussion-based online medium. By reading student end-of-course surveys each week, speaking with academic counselors and talking to students at graduation each year, I found that the instructor's performance in the following areas seems to tie closely to perceptions of their effectiveness: (1) *visibility*, (2) *feedback*, (3) *materials* and (4) *retention*.

Consequently, effective training programs focus largely upon these areas. Specifically, they teach online instructors to (1) maintain visibility, (2) give regular feedback, (3) provide high-quality materials and (4) remove obstacles to student retention.

Even experienced onsite instructors need training, coaching and mentoring in these areas to translate their effectiveness from the actual to the virtual classroom. Having seen how important these skills are, I am convinced that prospective online instructors should receive extensive training and mentoring in these areas before "flying solo." This training will prevent them from making avoidable mistakes that detract from their effectiveness as online facilitators.

As an added bonus, instructors who attain proficiency in the above four areas tend to receive the most positive feedback from their students and colleagues. They also enjoy the gratification and intrinsic rewards of helping students to fully grasp the class objectives and progress toward degree attainment.

This chapter will focus upon each of the topics mentioned, providing prospective, new and experienced online instructors with a thorough understanding of the importance of each aspect of online teaching and how to attain proficiency in each area. In each of the following four sections, I will share a vignette or two to illustrate the significance of the topic and generally discuss the components of each instructional competency. Finally, I will provide more specific examples and further explore the components that make up each of the four main areas of online instructional foci.

The Role of Visibility in Online Teaching

A few years ago, a new online teacher received negative feedback due to students' perceptions of his "low participation" in the class discussion. Students complained to an academic counselor that they only heard from the instructor at the end of each week's discussion. Since previous instructors had been more involved in class discussions, they wondered if their current instructor was lazy or uninterested. When their counselor suggested that they ask the instructor about their perceptions, the students did so with great trepidation for fear of offending the instructor.

While taken aback at their criticisms, the instructor explained that he was trying to avoid dominating the discussion; thus, he read each day's notes with interest, but saved his own remarks until the end of the week. He further described how he summarized the discussion, analyzed it in light of his experience and the readings, and extended upon the discussion to foreshadow the next week's lecture. The students agreed that his input was valuable, but pointed out that the relative sparseness of the input was discouraging to them, since they were used to more regular messages from their instructor.

The instructor finally realized what the problem was. The students could not "see" him reading notes and nodding his head encouragingly, or be aware of his presence on days when he did not write to the class. When the instructor fully understood the dilemma, he agreed to write more notes to the discussion meeting during the week. Soon, the students perceived that he was "visible," and his consistent presence reassured them that they were progressing appropriately. The students felt gratified that their feedback had been taken seriously and that it resulted in a positive resolution, since the instructor's accommodation to their needs as learners made their class more interactive and rewarding.

During an online mentorship, an instructor-in-training with full responsibility for an online class suddenly disappeared for a few days. His mentor tried to reach him by computer and phone yet was unable to get any information other than that the trainee was out of town on vacation. By the time the trainee finally resurfaced days later, his mentor had already stepped in and saved the class from derailing. When asked for an explanation, the trainee described how he had gone on vacation to another city, expecting to load the conferencing software onto his host's computer. However, he was unable to load the software. Even after he officially failed mentorship and was denied admission to the online faculty, the disgruntled trainee could not understand why being off-line and out of communication for a total of six days out of a five-week class was such a concern.

Lack of visibility and desertion of a class without communication to the administration does not bode well for an online instructor's willingness to put the students' needs first. Every online instructor needs to be aware of the various ways they can increase their visibility in their classes.

Online Visibility and Public Messages

The preceding vignettes point out that public messages are key to the perceptions of an instructor's presence. Similarly, since no one can sense someone's presence in an online environment, written messages from the instructor to students in the online class are necessary for students to feel connected in the online classroom environment.

On a related note, online instructors often do not realize that sending personal correspondence via the online medium does not substantially enhance their visibility. Namely, if instructors answer individual questions by replying to personal inboxes, other students fail to see the interaction; that is why conducting as much class business as possible in the open forum is recommended.

What kind of messages does a visible instructor send? A sampling of the variety available and examples of each include the following:

- Content-related messages (lectures, handouts, clarification of points in the text, discussion questions, synthesis of discussion)
- Process-related messages (order of assignments, directions for sending assignments, description of the flow of the class, guidance when students become confused)
- Technical tips (software tips, information about how to send attachments, discussion of how to format notes, URL's)
- Protocol guidelines (code of conduct, plagiarism statement, netiquette, online tone)
- Responses (answers to student questions, feedback on work submitted to the meeting)

If students benefit from visibly seeing the instructors' notes in the online classroom, which messages are particularly effective in establishing visibility? Messages demonstrating that the instructor is actively reading the discussion often prove effective. ("Canned" messages, although at times necessary, are somewhat less effective in establishing visibility because they do not represent individualized responses, nor clearly reflect that the instructor is involved in reading and responding to this particular class.)

As one technique that enhances the instructor's visibility while adding content-related value, some instructors remove the name from a question addressed to the instructor's personal box, share the question in the main forum and answer it publicly to benefit others in the class who may have the same question. In fact, the question may be from a student in another class being taught concurrently or even from a student in a previous class. The origin of the question does not matter, as long as the sender's anonymity is protected and students benefit from the instructor's response.

Online Visibility and Modeling

Another benefit of instructor visibility is that the visible instructor is modeling how the discussion-based instructional model works. If students are required to write to the meeting a certain number of times each week, for example, I would argue that online instructors should maintain at least the same level of participation as the students.

A key to setting a positive example is that an instructor modeling a high level of participation often motivates students to enhance their own participation. They know that the instructor demands their participation by observing the instructor's high participation level. On the other hand, when an instructor does not maintain an adequate level of participation, students may assume they have been given tacit permission to reduce their own levels of participation. They assume that their instructor will not feel comfortable confronting them or grading them down for the same behavior that the teacher is exhibiting.

Online Visibility and Reducing Isolation

A final reason that visibility is critical is to prevent a sense of isolation that distant students often encounter. If the students connect to the classroom once or twice a day, finding a number of new messages in the open forum each time, they feel reassured to be working collaboratively with their instructor, as well as other students. If they fail to see a note that they expected (e.g., a weekly lecture), they learn to react and ask the instructor directly for the materials that are missing. The comfort felt by students whose instructors are visible cannot be underestimated in the distance education environment, where students do not have the trappings of the traditional university (e.g., familiar faces, student unions and student activities) to provide a sense of belonging.

Ultimately, taking responsibility for being "visible" means that the instructor will alert necessary personnel if anything occurs that would prevent him or her from fulfilling his or her contractual obligation. If an emergency arises, the instructor should follow the university's procedures in order to ensure that the students' learning will not be interrupted. Often a substitute teacher is essential, due to the high need for instructors to be visible in the online classroom.

The Role of Feedback in Online Teaching

One neophyte online instructor whom I observed felt strongly that the university's focus upon regular feedback, particularly evaluative feedback, was exaggerated and that it distracted from the learning process. He told students that they would only hear from him if they were "heading for trouble." Otherwise, they should assume that they were doing fine. Only when he received several furious student end-of-course surveys after his class did he realize that his practice, while understandable and consistent with his teaching style, was neither appropriate nor effective from the perspective of his online students. Students stressed that they needed regular feedback to know how their performance was judged, how they could improve and how their final grade was calculated. The instructor discussed this situation with more experienced online facilitators and, with their assistance, adapted to his students' demand for substantive and frequent feedback.

Frequent and Consistent Online Feedback

Effective online instructors not only write to class meetings regularly, they provide frequent and consistent feedback to the class, as well as to individual students. Frequent and consistent feedback in the online classroom can stimulate active engagement with techniques such as questioning assumptions, disagreeing with certain points and pointing out well-analyzed points.

Of course, these facilitation skills are not dissimilar to those of an instructor in a face to face classroom; yet, the frequency and consistency of feedback are even more necessary in an online classroom. Why? Online students cannot see their instructors or other students nod their heads, frown, look quizzically, or smile encouragingly. What is usually nonverbal feedback must occur through written messages, which makes online feedback particularly critical.

Giving feedback in the main meeting includes asking questions, suggesting alternative perspectives to consider and extending on students' ideas. Feedback also includes answering questions in the main forum whenever possible, since many times the answer to one student's question may prove useful to the entire class.

Timely Online Feedback

Providing timely feedback within the class forum is important. Since an online class moves quickly, timeliness is essential to give students guidance and teach them the material in depth. Further, when guiding asynchronous discussions, the instructor needs to facilitate and foreshadow, instead of "catching up" with the discussions that have already been written and digested. Less timely feedback may lead to a perception that the instructor is not fully involved in the class, whereas timely feedback reassures students that the instructor is focusing upon them and their classmates' learning. Furthermore, feedback that is timely is far more motivational and beneficial to performance improvement than delayed feedback. Thus, online feedback is best when it is prompt.

Diplomatic Online Feedback

When feedback is provided to students in the main class meeting, diplomacy is essential. Since student motivation is closely linked to self-efficacy, well-worded feedback will encourage learners to continue in their programs and feel confident that they will succeed online.

Well-worded suggestions from the instructor are valuable not only for the student's learning process, but also may provide learning opportunities for the entire class. For example, gently pointing out the need to explore a theory underlying an opinion more fully may lead to the class's understanding that "gut feelings" are not convincing within the context of an academic discourse. The point can generally be made without undue embarrassment to the student who shared the gut feeling.

Occasionally, an instructor requests that students critique each other's assignments in the online classroom, usually providing guidelines for effective analysis to make the criticism constructive as opposed to personal or negative. When diplomatically worded, this type of feedback may also enhance the learning experience, since students practice the skill of receiving peer feedback, as well as the skill of providing critiques to their peers in a written forum. I am convinced that setting the correct guidelines to ensure that students are supportive, as opposed to attacking, is essential to the success of this technique.

When the instructor needs to provide critical feedback to individual students, the feedback should be couched in a way that maintains the learner's dignity. If a student is exhibiting behaviors that are disrupting the learning process, for example, he or she will need to receive positive but clear feedback that the conduct is not appropriate. The wording (and private transmission) of such a message will help to avoid further disruption in the learning environment by reducing the chance of the situation escalating. A critical message may need to be rewritten several times before the correct tone and wording are achieved; however, this attention to diplomacy is far more likely to bring about the desired outcome than sending a less reflective message.

Evaluative Online Feedback

One online instructor whom I coached became increasingly frustrated when students asked how she calculated grades for the course. Having worked with elementary school students for years, she was not used to being challenged about her grading policies and procedures by students. Fortunately, through our discussions she realized that grading was part of teaching and that doing it well would lead to more effective student learning. Further, by scoring students' work and tying it to the grading guidelines shared in her syllabus, she removed some of the ambiguity in her grading procedure and demonstrated to her adult learners that their performances matched the grades they earned. Additionally, after teaching more courses, she recognized that her students needed regular, detailed feedback during the course, not just a grade at the end.

Fortunately, she no longer needed to answer frequent questions about grading, since her new procedures and guidelines were clear and consistent, thereby allowing relatively little ambiguity.

Evaluating students is an important part of the providing effective feedback. As at any university campus, learning to fairly and effectively grade is a teaching skill that must be mastered by all online instructors to be successful.

Why should an instructor invest the time to provide detailed evaluative feedback to online students? Online students tend to have high standards for their own performances, especially if they are adult learners who have returned to school after succeeding in their work lives. Like any learners, they need to know where they stand in order to gauge how best to improve. Substantive feedback helps them to perform at higher levels and thereby earn higher scores in subsequent courses.

Students in an online forum, perhaps because it is a relatively young learning medium, may resist accepting an instructor's grading more than students faced with a similar situation in a regular classroom. This is even more likely due to the ease with which a student can send a quick electronic message, as opposed to the possible intimidation factor when addressing an instructor in person. Although often the most uncomfortable aspect of teaching, grading effectively is critical to student learning and effective online teaching.

What should an online instructor do to encourage students to understand the need for and utility of grades? One curriculum supervisor and online faculty member I know, compares the process of grading to that of evaluating employees when his students balk at his rigorous grading practices. Discussing grading in this context seems to help set the right expectations and attitudes when students fail to recognize that grading is unavoidable in most programs, not to mention that the instructor is the authority when grading disagreements arise.

Completing a weekly grading summary with point values helps both the instructor and student to recognize when a student needs help to succeed. If a student does poorly in a class and fails to improve with constructive weekly feedback, some advising may be necessary, such as a suggestion that the student consult an academic counselor.

Templates and Online Feedback

How is evaluative feedback delivered in an online setting? Universities establish their own guidelines and often articulate these in the instructor's contractual agreement. For example, many online programs require that specific feedback on assignments (including grades) must be provided within a week of the assignment's receipt. This specific evaluative feedback, as well as the use of weekly templates, helps students to understand how their grades are earned and to avoid surprises at the end of the course.

Experienced online instructors have often attested to the value of using templates when providing weekly feedback to students' personal boxes. Each individual student receives a completed template articulating the points they earned on assignments (out of total possible points), as well as points for each week's participation. A few sentences highlighting the student's performance, such as encouraging him or her to try harder the next week, are also highly recommended. Here is an example of a typical week's template:

Dear Jim:

Your point totals for this week are as follows:

__06__ of 06 possible points for discussion

__10__ of 10 possible points for participation

__17__ of 20 possible points for the week's essay

__06__ of 06 possible points for weekly summary

Your total is 39 out of 42 points. (Please use the past week's grading summary if you wish to compare your total points so far with the points possible and look up your grade so far in the course.) Also, let me know if you did not receive any of your assignments this week, as I returned them earlier this week with specific feedback and suggestions.

Jim, you showed a great deal of improvement in your participation levels this week, sending quality messages 6 out of 7 days this week, as contrasted

with 4 out of 7 days last week. I particularly enjoyed message #57, in which you outlined a situation at work and tied it to the theories in Chapter 4 of your text. I hope that next week you will continue to participate actively, since your well-considered questions bring up important points and add to your peers' learning experience at this online university.

Warmly,

Jill B. (Instructor)

Instructional Materials in Online Teaching

A seasoned instructor, hurrying to upload the syllabus and first week's lecture, failed to proof-read online materials that she had used many times to teach the same course. The due dates for assignments within the syllabus included various dates in April, although the class was running in June. After asking the appropriate questions to correct the situation, her students still expressed a high level of frustration with the instructor, having perceived correctly that she did not take the necessary time to customize her materials for the current class. The embarrassment that resulted made such an impression upon the instructor that she warned other instructors to revise their materials carefully and likely saved others from similar mistakes.

Content-driven Online Materials

Instructional materials include syllabi, mini-lectures, handouts, references to URL's and readings on the topic, assignments, discussion questions, examples, answers to assignments and other materials that are either pre-written before the class begins or added during the class to enrich the content of the course.

Messages that are not content-driven should be minimized, since discussions need to be focused upon the class and non-content messages may prove distracting to the topics being explored. While an instructor's role is to facilitate, it is also to provide supplemental material that enhances the text and thereby helps students to attain a deeper understanding of the course and to meet the stated learning objectives.

Carefully Edited Online Materials

The content expertise that is infused into a written online lecture, along with the chance to see examples of others' materials, can lead to a higher-quality presentation than typically seen in traditional classrooms. If, however, the instructor does not edit the materials carefully, the result may be an embarrassing situation, as shared in the vignette.

The ability to polish and improve class materials each time a class is taught is a huge advantage of online teaching over onsite. Of course, refining class materials demands that an instructor remembers to record when an assignment needs clarification or a point demands more elaboration next time. For future classes, the ensuing modifications directly benefit students, who are the recipients of increasingly polished materials (often worthy of publication).

If the university uses modules or course materials that are appropriate for a regular classroom, the instructor may be called upon to adapt the course to an online format. In cases like this, all of the oral presentations should be removed and group projects should take into account the time involved in coordinating group projects within an asynchronous medium. Modifications to an onsite module must be carefully communicated to online students in a timely fashion to avoid confusion.

Speaking with a colleague who teaches for a well-known online university, I asked how and when their curriculum developers adapted syllabi from the regular to online versions. She explained that the developers usually provided an online-specific version *after* publishing the onsite version. She also noted that the curriculum adaptations were not always successful, since the adapters were usually not online teachers, but editors. Once, in fact, the editors had missed something significant—proficiency in oral presentations was listed as a learning objective of a text-based online course. Even more tellingly, four group projects were due in a five-week online course. She and the other online instructors were forced to re-edit the curriculum so that it would work online. As a result, they suggested to the administration that future syllabi be adapted solely by experienced online instructors.

An instructor teaching a course for the first time may wish to contact previous teachers with curriculum questions or suggestions. At some universities, instructors are encouraged to share online syllabi and/or lectures as examples, although usually instructors develop their own lectures. This helps to personalize them and infuse them with their own content expertise.

Online lectures need to be concisely written, since they are not mere transcripts of oral lectures. Drawing upon text readings, work experience and outside sources, the online instructor crafts a thought-provoking and polished piece based upon the theories covered in the assigned readings. Further, online lectures may conclude with two or three well-placed discussion questions designed specifically to promote critical thinking and stimulate the week's discussion in the class forum.

Lastly, since Web addresses (or URL's) change frequently, a careful instructor always checks the URL's thoroughly before sending up a lecture that includes Web addresses. (The rationale for the use of URL's will be more thoroughly covered in the next section.)

Copyrighted Online Materials

Instructors may be tempted to send full-text articles from newspapers or the Internet to their classes, particularly if they are accustomed to handing out copies of articles in traditional classrooms. However, the practice of sending full-text articles without permission from the publisher is legally prohibited except for rare instances.

I encourage current and aspiring online instructors to share up-to-date and relevant materials by providing students with URL's instead of sending full-text articles to the online classrooms. This practice protects them and their universities from copyright issues.

Not only is the practice of providing URL's effective from a legal standing, it also encourages students to explore the Web. Students may be compelled to do further Web-crawling during or after looking up the cited articles, so the extra effort may prove helpful to their researching abilities.

As in regular classrooms, instructors may highlight and attribute short excerpts from published materials according to copyright laws. The 1997 booklet *Questions and Answers on Copyright for the Campus Community* by the Association of American Publishers, is an excellent resource for educators determining whether to cite a passage or refer students to URL's.

Orderly Online Materials

Posting materials on set dates helps students to get into the flow of an online course and program. If the university prescribes these dates, the students move forward in their programs without needing to readjust to each new instructor's timing. For example, students may learn to expect a weekly lecture, depending upon what the university requires. Similarly, they may anticipate that certain assignments, such as weekly assignments, are due on certain dates from course to course.

Other materials, such as handouts, need to be clearly highlighted by the instructor for maximum clarity and usefulness. Besides highlighting these materials, instructors may use branch meetings or otherwise distinguish the readings for clarity's sake. Further, students should be clearly informed whether reading each is mandatory or discretionary. This will enable the students to focus, organize and manage their time and support their success as learners.

The Online Instructor's Role in Student Retention

A student whose personal and professional life hit rough patches at about the same time felt depressed and generally pessimistic about her online studies. While she had been doing well and making solid progress toward attaining a diploma within a year, she felt that her focus was scattered and that she should "stop out" for a few months before returning to the university. She mentioned this to the instructor from whom she had taken her first online class. The instructor, who had been honored in the past for her teaching skills and commitment, spoke for half an hour on the phone with the discouraged student. Actively listening to the student's story, she asked questions such as "How would you know whether the time was right to return?" She also asked about the student's online cohort, whom she might miss at graduation if she needed to walk across the stage at a later date.

Upon reflection, the student decided that she wanted a predictable goal in her life, something that at times brought a sense of mastery, so she returned to complete her program. When she met her instructor in person for the first time at graduation, they hugged each other, and the teacher, seeing the fierce pride and joy of the graduating student, felt a renewed determination to support other students deciding whether to continue in their degree programs.

As mentioned earlier, online students may more easily feel isolated, since they are not getting the immediate feedback that their onsite counterparts enjoy. Instructors who help students to succeed are the best online teachers, particularly for teaching the first courses in each program. When students stumble, these instructors often reach out to encourage them and inspire them to continue with renewed confidence.

In my experience, online students who take a break during their programs, a phenomenon known as *stopping out,* may never return to achieve their educational objectives. That is why instructors who truly believe in education wish to help our students overcome obstacles to educational success and attain the goal they set out to achieve, which is an undergraduate or graduate degree.

Distance education traditionally poses a particular challenge to student retention. Researching why online students leave is even more difficult, since locating out-of-attendance students and then getting accurate answers about why they left are challenging obstacles to valid research on this topic. Yet, from my discussions and reading, the following factors appear to contribute to online attrition:

- Students leave because of isolation.
- Students leave because of the accelerated pace.
- Students leave because of competing responsibilities.
- Students leave because of technical issues.

Isolation and Online Retention

When a student is alone at a terminal, no matter how many messages she is seeing on the screen, the student may still feel alone. Why? A student may find it more difficult to develop the same informal relationships in an online environment that arise on-site, although mechanisms such as a student chat room and posting online bios at the beginning of each class may help facilitate camaraderie and student bonding. Further, a student might miss seeing other's nonverbal communications. When a student feels stressed, he or she might pull back from the group more easily, since the student will not "lose face" as openly as in an onsite classroom. This, in turn, may cause the sense of isolation to worsen.

The instructor should monitor all their students' participation and contact those who are not participating. Depending upon the situation, a phone call may prove more timely and effective in reaching a student who appears to be non-responsive to overtures from the instructor. Continued non-responsiveness may demand that the instructor involve the university's staff, depending upon the university's guidelines.

Accelerated Pace and Online Retention

Many online programs model an accelerated learning pace so adult learners can earn a bachelor's or master's degree while continuing to work full-time. When the pace is grueling, students may leave for what they think is a few months' break and then lose the momentum to return to school. Since students report that life never seems to slow down, the accelerated pace of an online program may be far more challenging than they initially anticipated.

Burnout is also possible, depending upon whether a student can cope with the demanding pace of reading texts, discussing online, researching, writing lengthy papers and completing study group projects. Particularly when time management is a challenge, students may procrastinate, begin to accumulate "incomplete" grades and then feel overwhelmed at the prospect of making up the uncompleted coursework.

Sharing time-management skills in the class, along with setting the evaluative criteria, providing regular encouragement and giving clear feedback about students' progress, will help to keep students encouraged through long nights of studying at a distance. Occasionally, I have found it helps to focus the student upon the pride they will feel as they graduate and then move the discussion to their "to do" lists and small accomplishments.

Competing Responsibilities and Online Retention

Most students who choose an online program do so at least in part for the flexibility offered by a distance education program. Not having to be online at a specific time is attractive to busy working professionals. Some students, however, confuse flexibility with lack of rigor.

For whatever reason, it may be easy for a student to underestimate the commitment required to complete the challenging coursework of an accredited online program. This commitment often involves delaying gratification in other areas of life in order to succeed in the degree program. Turning on the computer after an exhausting day of work and family responsibilities may prove daunting, particularly if a student overestimated the time commitment involved in participating actively online, as well as working on research papers and projects.

Even for students who knew what to expect when deciding to return to school, life might intervene and demand another analysis of school as a priority. For example, working adults are in the age range where they often face unanticipated work pressures (e.g., a downsizing or a promotion), as well as the dual demands of children and elderly parents. Any of these, particularly when a student is in an accelerated online program, may compete for attention with schoolwork and attainment of educational goals.

Students may consider withdrawing from a program due to feeling overwhelmed by work, home, or other responsibilities. Discussing with students the value of attaining their educational goals and helping them to prioritize will assist them in juggling their responsibilities while continuing to progress toward their educational objectives. Being flexible with deadlines is also an effective strategy. (For example, instructors often require that students must communicate with them before a deadline to arrange a postponement; those who do not do so are docked for lateness.)

Technical Issues and Online Retention

Occasionally, students encounter technical issues related to hardware, software and their levels of proficiency with either. If the students are relatively non-technical, the mystery involved in solving technical issues may seem overwhelming.

An online student prevented from logging onto the classroom compares to a regular student driving up to an educational facility to find the doors locked. If a student is unable to reach an online classroom, for whatever reason, it rates as an emergency that must be resolved quickly.

In the online classroom, issues related to software or hardware will likely arise. User issues can often be resolved by the online instructor or by other students in the class. Other issues may involve calling technical staff at the university or software vendor. In emergencies, instructors often help the students get the appropriate technical support that is so essential to the student's retention and success. For example, if the online university has a help desk that serves students and instructors with technical questions, calling the line for a student may help the student to receive more prompt attention and thereby decrease the probability of the student leaving the program.

Conclusion

Mastering the skills described in this chapter will bring online instructors the satisfaction of knowing that they can motivate, educate and retain adult learners earning their university degrees through the online medium. With practice and commitment, they will be gratified to find that their efforts increasingly prove effective in producing the desired learning outcomes of the courses that they teach.

As educators expand and polish their teaching repertoires in the online medium, experienced online facilitators will help to lead new instructors to successfully adapt to this flexible, demanding and dynamic learning environment. As part of this adaptation, online instructors should build upon the four areas of proficiency described in this chapter with fresh perspectives and innovative instructional strategies.

References

Kauffman, R. (1996). Assessing the virtual university. *Adult Assessment Forum*, Summer, 13-16.

About the Author

Anita received her doctorate in higher education from the University of California, Berkeley. She is former director of academic affairs at the University of Phoenix Online and Executive Assistant to the Vice-President of Academic Affairs at Ocean County College.

Chapter 5

MANAGING TIME

Developing Effective Online Organization

by Marilyn Simon

Time is one of our most valuable resources. It is important that we spend it wisely. The adage that "by planning for the future, we can live in the present," long accepted in the business world, has profound implications in the academic world, especially in the online environment. Online teaching and learning require more independent facilitating and learning than onsite courses, and substantially more time management skills

Time management includes good program planning where resources (people and time) can be used effectively. Daily work is made easier when a model provides a continuing guide for action, various levels of accountability and responsibility, and when essential tasks and sequences of tasks are specified along with a timeline for completion.

Both online learners and facilitators enter the learning environment with highly diverse life experiences. Life experience and prior educational experience have the greatest potential influence on learning. It is critical that programs of study be designed to organize new information in relation to the learner's prior knowledge and learning style, and to integrate new knowledge with existing knowledge.

Some people think best in the morning while others prefer the evening or afternoon. Online education affords you the opportunity to maximize your learning experience by selecting your own time to "be at school." It is important that the online student stays current with the work and asks questions to clarify any information that is unclear. However, it is important to know that online learning does not mean the student is totally self supportive. It is critical to be able to connect with other learners and faculty members, and to be aware of any online support services provided by the institution.

Online teaching is labor intensive. An online faculty member may be teaching two or three classes, taking part in a faculty development workshop, visiting the faculty lounge, mentoring another faculty member and reading massive personal messages that require response. How can he or she possibly make sense of all this information and still have time for a full-time job, a family and a life? Understanding time and information management can substantially assist the online faculty member to improve learning outcomes and preserve the precious resource we call time.

In the online classroom environment, most communication tends to be written. There is a high expectation that the student will be sending several messages everyday and that the facilitator will be responding in kind. This is a complex situation that can become overwhelming and lead to burnout, or at least to a low desire to face the computer everyday. Effective time and information management systems can be life preservers in this sea of information. This chapter will discuss ideas and methods that can assist members of the online learning community to improve time and information management skills

The Elements of Online Time Management

Many factors affect online time. First, the *subject matter knowledge* a faculty member possesses is inversely related to the amount of time needed to respond to queries by students. It is unquestionably easier to compose a response if one is an expert in the area they are facilitating. A faculty member with little real experience in a subject area will essentially have to learn as the course progresses and that can be quite time consuming. However, if a faculty member finds him or herself lacking expertise in a course, or is a bit "rusty," it would behoove the instructor to find a veteran faculty member to serve as a mentor. With permission, it would be wise to *lurk* in the mentor's online class. "Lurking" and "mentoring" are excellent means for any new online faculty to obtain the necessary online experience and to learn from a seasoned instructor.

Second, *keyboard skills* will largely determine time efficiency in a written communications environment until voice transcription technology becomes a more reliable alternative. Keyboard skills are a bottleneck anytime fingers on the keys cannot produce the written word as quickly as the mind can compose it. The goal here, as any good typist would say, is to learn keyboarding well enough to compose words and even phrases in whole (e.g., typing without having to spell words out in one's mind at the same time). The good news is that the more one types the better these skills become.

For years, the computer keyboard has been the dominant method by which words are converted from oral to written form. It seems a foregone conclusion that voice transcription will eventually emerge as the primary word processing data-entry interface. Such technology exists and it is rapidly improving. Although embracing voice transcription technology will require some short-term time investment, it promises to be a method that will improve long-term time-management skills. Those who will use word processing most productively in the future are likely those who have learned both excellent voice transcription skills as well as excellent keyboarding skills.

Third, *software applications and skills*—the ability to identify and use reliable, effective software—can be a major time saver. This allows the user to be able to cut and paste information and to move freely from one application to another. A database program that allows a faculty member to easily keep a record of individual student needs, work and grades is an invaluable resource.

Fourth, a *good database-management strategy* can help the instructor focus on the unique information elements and the relationships between these elements. This means having information readily available on each student's academic work, needs, background and interests in order to ascertain important information quickly. Taking the time to prepare a customized grade sheet template is a wise investment of time. It is critical that all assignments and correspondences are kept on file and that a copy of the syllabus be available whenever engaging in activities relating to the course. Keeping all this information in the same place, preferably by the computer, is a fundamental time saving measure.

Fifth, *reading efficiently* is a must. Most online courses—besides being completely textual themselves—are accompanied by a textbook(s) and other supplemental printed and electronic materials. There are skills that one can employ to assist learners to be more proficient readers. For example, the learner should take time to reflect on what it is he or she is hoping to find before they begin to read. If there are chapter summaries in a text, or an introduction to a chapter, reading this first could elucidate the information. The learner should be encouraged to relate the information to something already familiar.

Regarding efficient readers, it is a good idea to become familiar with the common academic writing models of disciplines and authors. These include the following:

- *Cause and Effect*: This takes place when the author explains a situation or theory and then delves into the consequences of its application. Cause and effect is prevalent in many sociology texts—for example, the author might describe the social learning theory and then describe a particular case, which exemplifies this study.

- *Compare and Contrast*: Here, the author examines two or more different theories or situations and their relationship to each other. Psychology texts which argue the Nature versus Nurture theory of child development often choose this type of presentation.
- *Process Description*: In this case, a certain concept, program or project is delineated and then examples are provided. Many texts that discuss total quality management present information in this manner.
- *Sequential*: This is when a case is built in a linear or historical manner. Analytical texts frequently use this style—for example, in learning about linear programming there is a step-by-step procedure that can be followed to obtain a solution.

It is extremely important that the online instructor helps learners to become active readers. This means asking questions like "What is the author's purpose? Why am I reading this? What conclusion does the author come to? Do I agree with this?"

Sixth, create a *working environment*. It is important that both the online facilitator and the online student create a place that is relatively serene and conducive for productive work. This special space should have the following luxuries:

- *Proper Lighting*. Poor lighting increases eye fatigue. Ideal lighting is indirect and free from glare. Many people find fluorescent lights to be easy on the eyes and free from shadows.
- *Proper Ventilation*. The brain needs fresh oxygen to function at its optimum. Keeping a window open would be an excellent way to satisfy this need.
- *Reasonable Quietness*. Try experimenting with soft classical or jazz music in the background and see if that increases your concentration and productivity. Having Mozart or George Winston music at a barely audible pitch is believed to increase higher ordered thinking skills such as creativity and critical reasoning.
- *Proper Supplies*. The are basic supplies and tools that you need to have in your working space, such as computer, modem, printer, textbook, syllabus, supplementary texts, clock, comfortable chair, telephone, surge protector and a Do Not Disturb sign. When the sign is displayed, it must be respected by others in the household.

Time Management and Student Feedback

Trying to respond to each correspondence by each student could grind you into pine-nut powder. It is important to resist the temptation of responding to everything and saving all notes. Selective responses are needed. Setting up a file for each student with important correspondences can be a useful time saving tool. Setting up a variety of meeting rooms and places to send correspondences is another organizing tool.

The facilitator sets the mood and climate for the learning environment. It is important that he or she be brief but courteous. When responding it would be best to quote the relevant passage, then highlight the message and add a response. *Cluttering* meetings with "I agree," "Me too," and "Thanks a lot" should be discouraged. This takes up a great deal of space and takes up valuable time. Constructive and pointed feedback is a timesaver and helps cut down on the amount of communication. It is important that a facilitator respond to personal questions within 24 hours if possible. A personal question could be an indication that a concept might need to be clarified for the entire class. A chat-room where students and faculty engage in informal discussions helps to free the rooms where the course information is explored and helps save time on getting to the type of information you are seeking.

Time Management and the Online Learning Curve

The learning curve effect is as real in the world of online teaching as it is anywhere else. If this is your first time teaching an online class, it is wise to start with no more than one class. Once you devise a study schedule and develop a routine, you will be able to add more to your online learning foundation.

On the first occasion, the time required to provide effective student feedback is always substantially more than the time it takes on the next occasion. Each subsequent feedback action requires less and less time. The same is true for the entire class facilitation process. Facilitating your first class effectively will require significantly more that it will take later on as you gain experience. Each subsequent class requires less and less time. In part, this is due to having a database of lecture notes, supplementary materials and templates that can be recycled and perfected over time. Although such time reductions are theoretically unlimited, it is a practical matter that the reductions at some point are no longer noticeable. Nevertheless, it takes many repetitions before improvements reach this point.

Decisions and Priorities

Managing time is a decision process. It is a set of decisions that recognizes time as a finite resource among tasks that are competing for this resource. An excellent first step in effective time and activity management is to write down your goals and the time that you need to complete each one. Next, it is important that you recognize other things that you have to do during this time. Look over the list and put a 1 next to the most important thing you need to accomplish and then number the other items relative to this list. Now break down each item into smaller chunks and make a weekly plan. First, fill in a calendar with all the time that you will be attending to your "have-to-dos". Next, fill in quality time that you can dedicate to your online courses. Choose something that you want to do that is not on the schedule and plan for that as well. Remember that allowing time for family and friends are crucial to maintain a fulfilling life.

Like many online professors, I wear several professional "hats." Besides facilitating online courses, I teach in traditional classroom settings in the evening, supervise research studies, conduct my own research and writing projects, and manage an educational consulting firm. I find that keeping an electronic calendar offers me the greatest flexibility and accessibility, and allows me to plan months, even years, in advance. Printing out daily, weekly and monthly schedules keeps me aware of current commitments.

I am a morning person. If possible, I try to do most, if not all, of my academic planning before noon and attend to my other professional responsibilities between 1:00 and 4:00 P.M. During a typical workday I will be out of bed by 7:00 A.M., answer my personal email messages before my first cup of coffee, complete some type of physical activity by 9:00 A.M., and then focus on my academic preparation. To set the mood, I turn on some music and sign onto my online classroom.

Once online, I respond to the most urgent messages in my personal mailbox. Once the fires are extinguished, I then check any assignments that are due on that day and move to the online classroom discussions. If a conversation is flowing smoothly, I will try to keep my two cents out of the discussion. However, if there appears to be a controversy or an impasse, then I will either offer my opinion or suggest means to seek a resolution. Once convinced that classes are flowing smoothly, I will then enter faculty discussions and bulletin boards. Usually 45 to 90 minutes is needed to accomplish these goals. The exception is on Thursday, when weekly grades are due. Generally, it takes 20 minutes per student for me to ascertain a weekly grade.

Effective time management is more than good technical skills. It requires appropriate priority decisions and flexibility. The time given to any task is the measure of its priority. Faculty members who devote 80 percent of their teaching time to the 20 percent of tasks and activities that really matter are the faculty members who are consistently successful in the classroom. Identifying "what matters" is the key to this process. Academic achievement is the objective when teaching. What constitutes the 20 percent that really matters when pursuing this goal in an online teaching or learning environment are issues directly related to student learning.

Time Management and Online Student Expectations

It is imperative that one set up reasonable expectations and then fulfills them. The course syllabus and other curriculum materials will set the basic classroom expectations. This includes how many times a week a student is to be online, how many times they need to respond to a discussion question, when assignments are due and what they need to accomplish to obtain a certain grade. From this basic set of expectations a faculty member must explicitly consider how they can best assist students in fulfilling these expectations. It is imperative that students know how to obtain support, where they can locate information, how they are to deliver their assignments and what the expected length of each assignment is. "Customers" are satisfied when expectations are met. A major element of the online instructor's job is to set appropriate expectations and then deliver the goods on time. Anything less will generate distractions from the primary academic achievement objectives.

A good syllabus serves as a scaffold for the course and clearly explicates when assignments are due and how they are to be presented, as well as provide hints for how to manage time. A complete syllabus should be sent prior to the first day of class and then weekly updates should be sent at the start of each week. Lowther, Stark and Martens (1989) found that obvious items are often omitted in syllabi. The major content areas of a comprehensive online syllabus are course information (description and objectives), instructor information, text information (readings and materials), course calendar and schedule (due dates, exams and special events) and course policies (attendance, participation, academic honesty, grading and support services).

Following is an excerpt from an online course syllabus in quantitative analysis. Notice that the due date, the approximate length of each assignment and what is expected of the student are delineated along with hints on how to effectively manage time.

1. *Reading Assignments*

   Read Chapters 4 & 5 in *Statistical Techniques in Business and Economics* and the corresponding chapters in the Study Guide. Each chapter is composed of four sections. You might wish to read two sections a day to stay current with the material and to allow yourself time for reflection. Keep a record of any concepts that you find confusing and need further clarification on. Post these to our main meeting room as needed.

2. *Chapter Assignments*

   Complete the Chapter Assignments found at the end of Chapters 4 & 5 in the Study Guide. Submit your assignment to my personal mailbox by Day 6. It might be useful to complete the material pertinent to each section as you complete that section.

3. *Quiz*

   Complete the Quiz provided on Chapters 1 – 3 (this is last week's reading) and submit this to my personal mailbox by Day 4. Do might wish to do this before you begin delving into the new material.

4. *Application Paper*

   Last week you chose a topic you wish to research which is of professional or personal interest to you. This week you need to find a professional peer-reviewed journal in your field (or a field that you are aspiring to enter) and a lay journal such as *Newsweek* or *Time*, and locate research studies related to your topic which uses and abuses statistics. In week 3, I will send you specific guidelines on how to evaluate these studies. The studies you choose need to have a significant amount of numerical data and at least one of them must have had a hypothesis that was tested using statistical hypothesis testing. Online journals are acceptable. If you have any difficulty locating such manuscripts, you might try conducting a web search or your local university library, if possible. If this is not fruitful, please send a note regarding this matter to my personal mailbox. The completed paper is due at the end of Week 5 and should be between five and seven screens in length. Submit a brief update on your progress on locating these studies to our "application" meeting by Day 6.

5. Discussion Questions

Please provide a brief response to the following questions and submit to our "main" meeting by Day 2. Respond to at least three submittals from others by Day 5.

Why do many people believe that "statistics is sadistic?"

How can knowledge of statistics change this belief?

6. Weekly Summary

Please prepare a weekly summary discussing the material you found beneficial this week. Submit your one- to two- screen response to the "summary" meeting by Day 7.

Time Management and Online Classroom Problems

Solving classroom problems can be very time consuming. Online classroom problems are often a result of students who believe they are not receiving appropriate feedback and or a result of some expectation that has not been met. As soon as a faculty member becomes aware of a classroom problem, it becomes his or her responsibility to deal with it. In the long run, it will save time if you give top priority should to preventing classroom problems. Learning from past experiences helps to prevent future problems.

An online student with a negative attitude can drain energy and time from the class. It is important that the online facilitator deal quickly with a student who is excessively contrary and appears to be dragging the class down. A phone call might be necessary to get to the root of the problem. In extreme cases, it might be beneficial to notify an academic advisor to encourage the student to reconsider their decision to take this course.

Preventing and Anticipating Technical Problems

The chief risk to electronic information is hard-disk failure. A hard-copy backup is the least technologically dependent. This is an information strategy that is rapidly declining in use as computer power and computer skills increase. The hard-copy strategy essentially revolves around printed pages and some form of file cabinet organizational techniques. Implementing this strategy is as simple as printing anything identified as potentially relevant for future use. The advantage of the hard copy strategy is that printed information is not subject to the whims of computer hardware (e.g., hard-disk failure). Hard-copy information management strategies are also by far the least difficult to implement requiring no more than printing or photocopying the desired data or documents.

One disadvantage of the hard-copy strategy is that printed information is retrieved manually. Unless great pains are taken to produce a functional index to the printed pages, then retrieval is often a matter of physically leafing through folders. Another disadvantage of the hard copy strategy is the need to reenter data when it is needed again in an online environment. It also kills trees.

Although hard-copy is a low-risk information management strategy, the future of this strategy seems doomed as the restrictions of the hard-copy approach make it completely inefficient. Information proliferates rapidly in an online environment that forces online teachers and learners to use electronic information management strategies.

A Final Thought about Time

Imagine that you had a bank that credits your account each morning with $86,400 and carries over no balance from day to day. Every evening it deletes whatever part of the balance you failed to use during that day. What would you do with such an account? Most likely you would make certain that you spent every cent every day.

Are you surprised to learn that you have such a bank? It is the TIME bank.

Every morning, it credits us with 86,400 seconds. Every night it writes off, as lost, whatever you have failed to spend or invest wisely. It will not carry over a balance. It does not allow for an overdraft. Each day, it opens a new account in your name; each night it erases the balance you had. If you fail to use the day's deposits wisely, the loss is profound. If you can invest about 10 % of this resource each day, for your online courses, you will be able to receive major dividends in your teaching and learning stock.

There is no drawing against the "tomorrow." No matter how wonderful your time-management skills are, you cannot get more than 86,400 seconds in a day. You must live each day on your daily deposit, invest it wisely to get from it the utmost in health, happiness and success from your personal and professional life! The clock is ticking. Make the most of each online day as well.

References

Lowther, M.A., Stark, J.S., & Martens, G.G. (1989*). Preparing Course Syllabi for Improved Communication.* Ann Arbor: University of Michigan, National Center for Research to Improve Postsecondary Teaching and Learning.

About the Author

Marilyn has a Master's degree in mathematics from Illinois Institute of Technology and a Ph.D. in mathematics, education and technology from Walden University. She teaches for Walden University, the University of Phoenix, Baker College, Upper Iowa University and the University of Utah. Her publications include "Geometry: An Informal Approach," "Math Start," "I Can Do Math," "Test Preparation Mathematics" and "Mathematics and Computers." She can be contacted at msimon@waldenu.edu.

Chapter 6

COOKING UP A SUCCESSFUL CLASS

Adapting Courses for the Online World

by Shelia Porter

No longer is distance education the black sheep member of the academic family, read about only in advertisements in the backs of magazines, with "courses" consisting of letters and red-marked assignments exchanged through the mail. In fact, online education today is one of the hottest topics in academic communities and corporate America. With the increased attention, more and more effort, study and technology are being dedicated to making online education programs not only reputable, but also a preferred method of education for some.

Online courses are highly interactive, even though students and instructors often sit many thousands of miles apart. I have facilitated traditional onsite and distance courses for various institutions of higher learning since 1993. I have also trained and coached many online faculty members and have discussed many of these topics with them in private and group meetings. Many professionals from other institutions have shared their experiences with me. I will synthesize those additional experiences along with other anecdotal information that I have gathered in my professional and personal studies in this area. In this chapter, I share what I have found to be the crucial ingredients of a productive and successful online course.

(Some of the inquiries that need to be made during the development of the courses may, at first glance, appear to be moot points, given the directives or resources of institutions developing or converting courses for online delivery. I encourage all who are charged with such development to dare to challenge the existing paradigms when necessary. The process of determining what will work well in each specific online environment is analogous to the work of an experienced baker when moving from one climate to another. A basic cake recipe made in Florida at sea level with high humidity is very different from that same recipe in southwestern Colorado at a high altitude and very low humidity. For a truly delicious cake in both places, it is not a simple matter of mechanically changing the measurements. The baker must customize the adjustments of different ingredients and adjust the oven temperatures, baking time and sometimes even the size of the pans to end up with a cake that rises well, looks good and tastes great too.)

Bandwagons are always popular to jump on, especially ones that appear to have huge profitability. Online programs are not for everyone, however, and will leave a very bad taste if poorly developed or delivered. As you have read in previous chapters, facilitating an online class well is not a simple matter of typing up lecture notes and making them available to students on a web site. Similarly, developing an online class is not a simple matter of taking an existing class syllabus, typing it up and requiring students to type up their answers to be sent to the instructor by email.

Here is the basic recipe to follow when developing an online class. Remember, though, you will need to customize the specific ingredients to create a course that looks and tastes great not only to you, but also to the audience you will be serving.

One Part Course Content and Teaching Expertise

First, start with a cup of course design. Keep basic pedagogical principles, combined with real life teaching experience, in mind. Effective online courses tend to be developed by experts in their content areas along with professional educators who are conversant with accreditation requirements and sound pedagogical principles. The end product of the collaborative work is a written course guide often called a *curriculum module*. Modules outline the objectives for each class session, outline assignments, recommend a grading scale and provide faculty with suggested activities and assignment details to satisfy the objectives. Students receive an abbreviated module without the faculty notes. Individual faculty members create their own syllabi which incorporate the modules' guidelines and provide all other necessary information such as details of assignments, deadlines and grading criteria along with overall course grade weight of assignments.

It is a good idea for new online courses to have been delivered first to students at an onsite class. In that way, you can see what has worked well in practice, not just in theory. You then use the tried and true module from the onsite classes as the basis, or starting point, for the online class. You adjust it by adding one part of this, and another of that, to make it appropriate for the online environment.

For example, in a business law class I facilitate, students present oral analyses of adjudicated cases and current articles in the onsite classroom. In the online class, these same assignments exist, but students present a concise written analysis instead of an oral one, and answer questions the other students and I submit to explain points of interest. The exchange is not quite the same as answering questions posed immediately after the speaker stops talking. Everyone is required to participate in the discussions at least five days out of seven each week. But the result is a substantial amount of discussion by everyone who wants to discuss a specific case or article more. The discussion time is not limited by the agenda for the allocated class hour.

In both classrooms, my practice as a business attorney enables me to help students focus on the main concepts and laws they are likely to encounter in their work lives. My experience as a teacher enables me to understand how to best communicate with them without too much legalese and figure out how to best assess their fulfillment of the learning objectives.

Some institutions have a more standardized approach for online education, disallowing individual faculty creativity in how the main topics of each lesson are presented. That is, some institutions provide the lecture materials and discussion questions each week (in the form of written materials or videos), limiting the faculty member's role to fielding questions and grading work submitted. I have facilitated classes under both systems and have found the more creative approach to be most satisfying for faculty and students. It is also most effective in terms of providing students with a personalized approach to what might otherwise be viewed as a program not far removed from the early days of correspondence courses.

Second, add a dash of an optimally sized class. Online classes tend to function best when enrollment is between 9 and 13 students due to the high degree of interaction between students and faculty on an almost daily basis. Conducting online classes with fewer students often results in too little discussion and expressions of fewer differing perspectives. Conducting classes with more students creates an unwieldy burden of having hundreds of email notes to read and digest.

Third, blend in a half-cup of online classroom organization. When developing online classes, you need to determine whether daily, weekly or other periodic levels of interaction between students and faculty best meet the course objective. For example, do you want a course in which students all read the posted lecture and assignment notes, then send their assignments to the instructors' personal email boxes, or do you want the students to interact with each other? Or might a combination be best?

Each faculty member and student will have a personal mailbox for private communications. Each class will also be designed with an open forum meeting that the faculty member and all enrolled students will have access to throughout the course. Branch meetings or "threads," which instructors have the options to create, are typically used for the submission and discussion of specific assignments such as current article reviews, weekly summaries and final course project papers. Discussions are held in the open meeting and branch meetings or "forums." Many assignments are submitted to these open meetings. Online students learn from each other as well as from the instructor. Attendance and active participation are key components in the course design and grading criteria.

Many online instructors organize their classes in the following way:

- *Main Meeting or Forum*: Students log into this meeting on the first day of class and use it for the majority of their discussion notes about assignments.
- *Lecture Hall*: Faculty members post their syllabi, lecture notes, assignment notes and other important notices in this read-only branch meeting (the software prohibits anyone other than the faculty member from posting notes here).
- *Article Reviews*: Many of the online classes include assignments to review and analyze current articles on topics raised in the textbooks.
- *Weekly Summaries*: Weekly summaries describing application of one or more of the main lessons learned are posted and discussed in this branch meeting.
- *Chat Branch*: Students and faculty use this optional branch meeting for non-course related topics.

Fourth, add a cup of technological expertise—use "just the right amount of technology." Do not lose sight of the basic pedagogical principles when tempted by technology and all it has to offer to add pizzazz to the design and delivery mechanisms for courses. It can be very tempting to build in lots of video clips, for example, or graphics, but ask whether they add to or detract from the focus of the course. How much time will students spend downloading and reviewing video or audio clips? Is that the best use of their time, particularly if the clips add little to the text or other written messages?

Similarly, what about the time students may spend adding to the font size and color of the text in their own messages, or even adding animation? Fancy fonts, colors and animation are fun and exciting, but if someone is pressed for time, I would rather have him or her spend it mastering the material rather than making the form of the message fancier. Additionally, keep in mind that not all students have state-of-the-art equipment. Thus, the use of technology must balance with practicalities.

At times, however, the use of advanced technology is only wise. The adage *A picture can paint a thousand words* is applicable here. In many situations, supplementing a narrative with a diagram or graph can help explain the message more clearly. Nevertheless, if you are going to ask students to use graphics in their assignments, consider whether they will need to dedicate inordinate amounts of time to the look of the assignment and the selection of the graphics. The result could be skimping on the content of the assignment. Be certain that everyone can view any graphics that you or the students create.

In other words, clarify the objectives of not only assignment content, but also assignment presentation as well as course design. Keep those objectives in sight when writing the details of activities. Do not encourage the use of advanced technological features if their use will substantially detract from time dedicated to the content of the course.

Choosing the Bets Software

Online educators today have numerous software options and software will continue to evolve, and because it would be inappropriate to mention only a few by name, I will outline the characteristics that have proved to be not only "must haves" but those that are greatly advantageous as well. You can make your own educated choices based on what is available when you are ready to develop your online courses.

"Must have" features for software include (1) it must be affordable, easily installed, easy to learn basic features such as reading, writing and sending notes; (2) it must run well on affordable computers (i.e., ones that most students and faculty are likely to have, generally not the latest, fastest, fanciest computers on the market); (3) it must have the ability to move and export notes singly or in groups; and (4) it must have the ability to create branch meetings or threads off the main classroom forum for specific assignments and discussions.

"Nice to have" features include (1) both offline and online readers; (2) built-in viewers to allow users to read attachments in various formats, such as PowerPoint, Excel, Word Documents, and so on; (3) different size and color fonts, as well as features such as underlining, bold and italics for text; (4) the ability to sort notes by sender and subject; and (5) the ability to embed hyperlinks into lectures and other notes to allow easy access to Internet sites.

Regardless of the software used, my experiences conducting online classes and training faculty have convinced me that irrespective of the level of computer user sophistication, students and faculty alike experience many frustrations when left totally on their own to learn the specific program software. Consequently, some orientation to your software needs to be provided to students as well as to faculty to help them be successful in the classroom. Additionally, training for faculty in online facilitation skills will help greatly.

Video and Audio Supplements

Some institutions use only text formats for class activities. Although there is no voice component in most online classes, there is always the option of calling each other on the phone as necessary, to clarify something instantly, or to defuse a situation that needs immediate attention. Additionally, some online class modules are accompanied by videos to supplement the text. Still others utilize texts supported by websites that provide updates and supplemental activities. So remember, combinations of technologies can work well and recommendations (or even requirements) for their use can be built into the curriculum to honor different learning styles.

One Part Financial Expertise

First, begin with a cup of financial investment in the design. Seriously consider the financial costs of design. Could teams of developers working together develop the course best? For example, the basic objectives, lecture areas and assignments could be outlined by a content expert—someone who has successfully taught the class in a traditional classroom. It would also be best to have that same person, or a co-developer, be experienced in a facilitative style of online teaching. As you have already read, simply providing a typed lecture for the online classroom does not work well. The instructor needs to pose questions that stimulate thought and that promote lateral learning. In the online classroom even more than in the face to face classroom, the instructor is most effective when she or he is the "guide on the side rather than the "sage on the stage."

Second, add a pinch of someone who understands the abilities and limits of the method of delivery. Such a person can provide incredibly valuable assistance at the course development stage. After all, it would be disastrous to give assignments that require students to submit charts or graphs if the software will not allow the transmission of them. On the other hand, if all assignments are limited to written reports, but the software allows the transmission and viewing of PowerPoint or other presentation software slides, you would be unduly limiting the creativity of submissions if you did not allow that method of assignment completion without good reasons.

Third, throw in a tablespoon of financial costs of equipment and software for the school, instructors and students. The major cost of computer equipment for an online education program may not be borne by the institution providing the program. The classrooms exist in cyberspace, so there are development costs for the class and for the server or Internet service that collects and redistributes all the electronic messages instructors and students create. However, the traditional areas of cost savings to the school are great because there is no real estate to be bought and no real property taxes to be paid for the classrooms.

This does not mean the classrooms are totally free for everyone. Unless you are going to be the extremely rare institution that provides computers to all faculty members and students, and pays their telephone and Internet connection costs, there are costs in the form of computers and Internet access, though some of this can be reimbursed. Your institution may be able to afford whatever computer equipment it needs for the support staff and administration, but not all students or instructors will be able to write checks for unlimited amounts. Keep these costs in mind as you develop courses.

Also keep in mind the cost of connection and specific course software. Will you be providing it free to students, or will there be an extra charge for it? Next, you need to know what other software is compatible or will cause conflicts while operating. For example, the release of Windows Vista raised these kinds of concern. Provide instructors and students with information about what to do (other than panic) when they experience such situations.

Develop a profile of the minimal, basic configurations of computer equipment necessary. For example, let students and faculty members know about recommended or required computer speed, memory, graphics capabilities and drives. In addition, consider how you will assist students and faculty to gain proficiency with the connection software. Will they learn it from manuals? Will your institution provide a web-based tutorial? What technical support will you provide?

Finally, make it clear to faculty and students the technical support faculty members are expected to provide students. An entry course is useful for undergraduates when it combines readings and discussions about skills necessary for beginning college degree studies as well as how to master use of our software. Although students are strongly encouraged to take advantage of a technical orientation, not all do. Faculty members in beginning courses need to provide software assistance and to allow for a sharp learning curve in the first two weeks. Later courses, however, can safely jump right into the contents of the course on the first day.

One Part Email and Writing Expertise

Messages, of course, are conveyed by much more than the words themselves. For example, if I write to a student, "I can't believe you wrote that in response to my last question," that message would most likely be read very differently from, "I can't believe you wrote that in response to my last question. :-)"

In the former instance, the student might be concerned that I did not agree with or approve of what she or he had written. In the latter example, however, the student would have a visual clue that I was OK with what was written. I am not ordinarily a "smiley-face" type person, but I have found that using a few selected emoticons in the online classroom is helpful. Online instructors need to come across as complete people, not just the ones making assignments and grading them. Emoticons help create a relaxed environment at appropriate times. By the same token, when I have a serious message to deliver, such as, "I haven't received your assignment that was due yesterday; please contact me ASAP," I do not want to inappropriately insert a smiley face even if I am tempted to convey a friendly tone. In other words, developers should know that it is imperative when designing online courses that someone needs to be assigned to work with faculty to help them understand the ways in which they can often supplement online messages.

In addition, online *tone* is important. Experienced users of email messages are often fans of brevity. A brief, to-the-point note can be read much differently than it was intended, however. For example, if I am concerned about how a student is doing and about whether I have received all assignments, the following note to the student is assured to elicit a different, more negative reaction than the second one:

Bill, I don't have your completed assignments that were due yesterday. Send me proof you sent them in on time, or let this note serve as your notice that you have earned an F for them.

Wouldn't you rather receive the following?

Bill, I don't have your completed assignments that were due yesterday. Perhaps I inadvertently overlooked them, or they didn't

yet make it to the right meeting? Please let me know when you sent them in, and if you don't see them in the main class meeting, please re-send them ASAP and let me know what happened. Of course, if you didn't send them in before today, please let me know that too and then send them in ASAP to obtain at least partial credit for them. (Please see the syllabus for partial credit for late assignments.)

Giving the student the benefit of the doubt, acknowledging when there might have been a misunderstanding, asking for clarification instead of making assumptions and allowing others to save face all form the foundation of proper online tone. A *please* here and there often help, too. Although these may be commonsense options for some, they are not in the forefront of the consciousness of many online developers and instructors, especially when writing email messages. If there is not going to be specific training about these communication skills for faculty and for students, some coverage of them in the modules and other course materials may help keep them on the right track and working productively together.

It may not be fair to expect perfection in every single message sent to every single mailbox, but it is reasonable to incorporate standards for written communications. The module or syllabus should clearly state the expectations of writing perfection in the daily class notes. Of course, it should go without saying that the modules should be free of typos and other grammatical errors, as well. Remind faculty to proofread their own syllabi, lectures and other notes to practice what they teach in all daily messages.

One Part Accreditation Expertise

I mentioned this part of the recipe briefly at the beginning of this chapter, so I will just briefly re-emphasize it here. It helps to have someone on the development team at least review the proposed course design and compare it with the requirements of the appropriate accrediting body. The last thing you want is to have a course ready to deliver, only to determine later that it is missing an important element or deficient in a required area.

Begin with a dash of legal expertise and beware of both sides of the copyright coin. Of course, no one wants to turn course development into a complex legal matter. Nevertheless, some basic information about important intellectual property issues may save you lots of time, energy and money later. There are many other legal issues that may be relevant and nothing in this section should be construed as legal advice, so, as in any situation, if you have specific legal questions or concerns, do consult an attorney. You may want to consider the following issues:

- *Clarify ownership of the course.* Always have a written agreement between the people actually developing the course and the institution for which it is being developed. It should state who owns the course as well as other crucial terms such as amount and timing of payment for the development. A common myth is that the author of a creative work always has the right to use the work or to copy it. The law, however, distinguishes between the rights of an author and those of the copyright owner when a work is created for another. The safest practice is to put the express agreement in writing, so the intentions are understood from the very start.

- *Honor others' copyrighted material.* One of the unfortunate byproducts of access to computers and familiarity with the Internet is that it is easy, and for some, tempting, to copy materials created by others. In the USA, in general, the creator (or employer of the creator when the works are "works for hire") automatically owns the copyright to original works "fixed in a tangible medium" even when there is no notice of copyright shown on the work. So, when in doubt, assume that copyright laws protect work created by someone else. That means it is not legally permissible to copy pages or parts of pages from the Internet or other sources. Institutions need to make it clear that those who are developing courses for them are to be the authors of original work they provide to the institution, or if they are not the authors, they are to provide written permission to copy from the copyright owner. (There are "fair use" exceptions to the copyright laws, but these must be carefully examined on a case-by-case basis for materials one is going to use under this provision of the law. Chances are that for repeated use in a course, the fair use exceptions will not protect the institution.) Developers and faculty members need to know that not only can institutions be held liable for copyright infringement; the individuals causing the institution to use the infringing materials can also be held liable under federal civil laws. In just the right circumstances, criminal prosecutions can result, as well.

And a Cup of Marketing Expertise

What good is a course if no one knows you offer it and if no one understands it is a part of a "real" degree program? Despite the fact that I spend the majority of each weekday in an online environment, I regularly talk to people who have no idea what we do at the online campus and who still question whether it is as good as traditional education. Marketing the program consists not only of efforts to sell it, to obtain students, but to educate others about the program as well. Marketing professionals can best market what they understand and have personally experienced. Consider providing them with information or a firsthand look at how an online class operates in practice, not just in theory.

Not only can marketing professionals help promote your courses but they can provide the developers with information about what potential students are looking for and expecting. Use their information when you design courses. They may help lead the content and teaching experts in an exciting direction. The overall efforts of marketing experts are an integral part of the recipe.

Conclusion

As you can see, the good news is that you can develop interactive educational courses utilizing current technologies for delivery; the bad news is that it is not as simple as typing up existing class materials. Developing or adapting a great online course is not an impossible task, however, if you have the right ingredients.

About the Author

Shelia earned her Juris Doctor degree from the University of Colorado in 1984. She is a former instructional specialist at the University of Phoenix Online.

Chapter 7

GETTING READY

The Syllabus & Other Online Indispensables

by Marilyn Fullmer-Umari

The online class room addresses the concern that Oxford University's business school dean, Douglas Hague, expressed about business schools not "delivering education that meets the needs of changing times, i.e., instantly available, instantly tailorable to increasingly divergent student needs." This chapter will examine the role of the syllabus and lecture as the foundation to fulfill the mission of high quality online instruction.

As an online instructor, I frequently receive questions about this method of instruction. Among the most frequently asked questions from faculty, friends and colleagues who hear about online are:

- Does an online syllabus differ from a traditional syllabus? How?
- What are the necessary elements of an online syllabus?
- How does an instructor gain and maintain high levels of attention and involvement from students who are reading an electronic lecture in the absence of gestures, animation and other visual cues?
- How do you illustrate instructional points in the absence of traditional classroom visual aids?
- How does an instructor decide how long a lecture should be?
- How, in the absence of visual cues, does an instructor understand if a student comprehends the lecture?
- Are there any pitfalls that I should avoid in preparing my online lecture?

Preparing the Online Syllabus

The syllabus establishes the course guidelines and is the basis for a successful learning experience. The first contact that the online student will have with the instructor is the online syllabus. Through the syllabus, students receive class information about the instructor, course learning objectives and topics, the schedule of reading and written assignments, and information about course expectations and policies. There are several factors that are of particular importance for the design of your course syllabus:

1. Class size. An online class of adult learners presents a wonderful opportunity for sharing by classmates and subsequent horizontal learning. Variations in class size, however, will directly influence requirements for participation, use of branch meetings and note management. In the onsite class, a larger class size requires effective facilitation to promote a balanced discussion among a greater number of students. As the number of students in an online class increases, the same expectations of participation will result in a proportionately higher number of notes for students to read and assimilate. This can become overwhelming and detract from a well-paced class environment.

In addition to reducing the number of days that students are required to participate in the class, expectations regarding maximum note length should be clarified at the outset as class size increases. Students should also be instructed to download notes more frequently in larger classes to stay caught up with the class discussion. Finally, establishing branch meetings for the instructor's lectures, homework and non-course related conversation becomes more important in larger classes. For example, I create a meeting that I call the "Class Lounge" to facilitate my ability to maintain a focused discussion of course topics in the classroom while not discouraging the students' needs to socialize and build relationships. The influence of class size on these aspects of the online classroom can be addressed as modifications to the syllabus.

2. Technology. The technology available to your online students creates important considerations for your scheduling of assignments. You should take advantage of the learning opportunity presented by this technology for both the timing of reports and projects as well as providing a well-sequenced schedule of increasingly challenging assignments. The instructor's syllabus should reflect a sequence of assignments that will give students sufficient time to learn the online methods. The level of student competencies in data acquisition and use of electronic tools will vary broadly. Moving too quickly into technologically complex requirements can result in students needing to spend excessive time learning the technology and less time preparing the actual project.

Appropriate integration of technology into class assignments can assist students in learning the skills that apply to the workplace. Course requirements, when used effectively, will support students' workplace performance. The starting point for designing assignments is to assess what level of skills students really need. As one student commented to me at the end of our class, "While I was reluctant at first to try using media that I was unfamiliar with for my assignments, the requirements for the final course project forced me to explore new methods and has made me a more valuable contributor at work now in the preparation of reports and presentations."

The syllabus for students taking their first online class will need to anticipate and address the higher level of uncertainty that students experience as they begin working in the online classroom. The focus in the first course should be on mastery of the technology used in the online program. Courses should introduce students to the Internet and the Web, offer resources that are relevant to the course, give information on how to conduct searches, and, depending on the technology of the course, instruct students to develop their own personal web pages. For courses early in the program sequence, I instruct students to research and submit a list of ten resources that can be used as references for future work in our class. This assignment allows me to assess the students' familiarity with the information environment available to them on the Net and the Web. A systematic approach to integrating technology into your courses will enable you and your students to effectively utilize available tools rather than being overwhelmed by them. Based on your specifications, students will submit assignments that may include spreadsheets, audio and video attachments, pictures and other electronic learning aids. It will be important for you to have clearly identified objectives for using these tools so that their inclusion does not become "entertainment" focused.

3. *Class sequence and course length.* The syllabus should present a schedule of the readings and assignments distributed over the course to allow adequate time to cover each area. Match readings and class assignments to support learning objectives. Keep in mind that online education is already a reading-intensive medium and you may want to reduce reading assignments slightly in comparison to the onsite classroom. For entry-level students, it will be especially important to have all assignment requirements clearly outlined in the syllabus.

4. *Well-designed course objectives.* While two of our purposes are to convey information and knowledge and to create a learning experience pertinent to the subject at hand, the online instructor must do this through the selection of assignments appropriate to adult learners and the online medium. The selection of each assignment should not only support course objectives but also recognize the strengths and limitations of the online classroom, and the preference of adults to take responsibility for their learning experience. For example, while adults value horizontal learning that study groups provide, the online medium must take into account time zones and turnaround time required for asynchronous discussions and assignment preparation.

5. Degree of course flexibility. Many online students are attracted to the program because they cannot be in an onsite classroom each week due to travel or other schedule conflicts. The appeal to online students of being released from the requirement to be in a classroom at a certain time and place on a regular schedule should be kept in mind regarding due dates for assignments.

In preparing the course syllabus, instructors should evaluate how important it will be to the mission of high quality instruction in their online classes that students submit assignments on a specific due date. To best meet the needs of many online students, it is desirable to offer some flexibility. I do this whenever possible by providing target due dates but also allowing additional time to submit assignments without penalty.

6. Setting the tone. In the onsite classroom, the instructor's appearance, voice and comments can help to establish the tone for the course. Similarly, online instructors use their syllabi to set the tone for their virtual classrooms. Decide on the degree of formality/informality that you want for the class and present your expectations in your syllabus regarding classroom climate. This can be accomplished by including the instructor's availability online and offline to assist the student, evidence of some flexibility and willingness to work with students, expectations for a professional tone and conduct in the class, as well as a demonstration of the instructor's willingness to be open. This sharing can begin by including brief biographical sketches at the opening section of the syllabus. As one student offered: "My experience so far is that most instructors are very open about themselves and their past experiences. This helps in providing a trusting and supporting environment where the people in the class can get to know each other and are able to communicate effectively as a class."

Elements of an Effective Syllabus

This section presents a list of essential elements that are required for an online syllabus. While some requirements are obviously more important than others are, this list provides a solid foundation for the outline of your course.

1. Course description and overview. The course description and overview provides an introduction to the subjects that will be examined in the course. As students read this over, they are looking to see not only what will be covered but also which topics will stimulate their interest. This section is an opportunity to get students really connected to the class. Will the course description communicate the importance and relevance of the ideas to be covered to the students' lives? The instructor who understands adult learners and their needs will create a description that connects the course topics to the competency-based needs of adult learners. The well-designed online course overview will generate energy and promote student commitment to the course subject and medium.

2. Instructor biographical sketch. This will be your student's first look at who you are. The nature of your course will determine what your students will want to know about you. I use a slightly different biographical sketch for different courses so that I can share relevant academic and professional experiences without becoming too detailed. I also personalize my bio by sharing some of my interests and hobbies. I try to communicate information about myself that lets students know that I value an environment of open communication where students can feel free to share their opinions. I include some humor to show that humor is welcome as well in my class. I also share a story that models a willingness to take risks and to be open to new experiences. Most importantly, I try to demonstrate that I am committed to the possibility of each student in the class having an incredible learning experience as well as being a partner in our learning adventure. Many faculty members refer students to their own personal web pages where students can "see" their instructors.

3. Instructor contact information. The majority of student contact will come through the online meetings and email. I communicate to students that I care about them and make myself available to them by providing the best times to reach me offline by phone. I state clearly that they can expect to have all questions or telephone calls returned within twenty-four hours.

4. Schedule of readings and assignments. Your syllabus should include the reading and written assignments for each week of the course. This schedule allows students to anticipate their workload and plan ahead for potential time conflicts thus enabling them to keep pace with the class. Your schedule should recognize holidays and the potential travel and additional time demands associated with these events. While a student may be able to do an individual paper during a holiday weekend, it may be difficult for study group members to coordinate their schedules to complete a joint project.

5. Review of class policies. You may want to cover the following items when discussing your class policies.

- *Attendance.* Present either the school's general attendance policy or your own expectations regarding how attendance will be taken online and the policy regarding absences. For example, attendance may be counted as logging on at least once during the class week. If the student does not log on during that period, an absence is recorded. The syllabus should state the number of allowed absences in a class and the affect, if any, on the student's grade.

- *Grading*. The syllabus should also include a clear statement of the grading policy and the timing of instructor feedback. Provide an outline of the requirements for each assignment and the relative weighting of points. You may also consider including a statement regarding how grade disputes will be handled.
- *Participation*. The policy regarding participation requirements is a critical aspect of the syllabus. Your policy should emphasize both the importance of participation to the learning experience as well as how participation will contribute toward the student's grade. My participation policy states both the level of activity that I am looking for in terms of frequency of participation as well as offering suggestions for contributions. Here is a sample of an online policy on participation:

Class, I want you to know that I'm going to facilitate our discussions in a way that I hope will make this an outstanding learning experience. I'll share my own views and examples. I'll offer questions about your comments. I'll try to generate mini-debates so that we really examine these issues from different perspectives. I invite you to question me, challenge me and certainly don't hesitate to disagree with me.

If a favorite topic or question doesn't come up, please take responsibility for generating a discussion on that. If you want me to address a topic that I haven't covered, simply ask the question. This is your class. You can help to generate the learning experience that you want by your own involvement. Each of you has a valuable contribution to make. Don't wait for the topic to come up or be asked to share an example. Jump in. The more involved you are and the more you take ownership in our class, the richer the learning experience will be for you.

Also, we could talk about any subject each week, but I encourage you to stay with our planned sequence and rigorously discuss and examine the material that is the focus for a given week. You will find that the continuity that this focus creates will open possibilities for higher quality discussion. In terms of grading your participation, I'll be looking for substantive and insightful examination of our week's topics on five of the seven days each week. A total of five points can be earned for each day of participation.

- *Tone in the classroom.* The comments from my students again and again refer to how much they enjoy and learn from our class discussions. The level of activity and quality of the participation will determine the quality of the class. The syllabus can set expectations for a respectful and professional tone in comments and feedback. I also encourage students to avoid sarcasm since the inherent negative effect of sarcasm is amplified in the online medium.

- *Late assignments.* You need to decide how you will handle the submission of late assignments and state that in the syllabus. Will late assignments be accepted? If so, will there be any penalty in the form of reduced points for late assignments? How will due dates be adjusted for students in different time zones? Will late papers from students who experience system difficulties also be treated as late in terms of penalties?

- *Exams.* Many onsite instructors give students "take home" exams. Similarly, online students can complete exams at home and submit them at a specified time to their instructors. Some schools may require a proctored exam for a midterm or final whereas other schools may permit all exams to be taken online. The syllabus should include your policy and schedule for exams to give students time to plan for taking the test. When I use exams in my online classes, I assign brief case studies which require students to apply course concepts in an analysis of the problems presented. I then can allow students to use their texts.

- *Academic dishonesty.* With some online resources making course papers available to students for a small fee or free, the problem of academic dishonesty is always present. The syllabus should present a clear policy regarding the seriousness of plagiarism, the forms of plagiarism and consequences for students in terms of course grade and academic status. The following is the policy of the University of Phoenix taken regarding plagiarism from the *Online Faculty Handbook*:

All the work submitted by a student must represent the student's original endeavor. Where outside sources are used as references, work submitted by the student should identify the source and make clear the extent to which the source has been used. Ideas or work presented in the private or public forums of the online electronic classroom are subject to the same standards of honesty. The University considers plagiarism and falsification of documents, including documents submitted to the University for other than academic work, a serious matter that may result in the following sanctions:

1. Failing grade for the assignment and/or course.

2. Suspension for a specified period of time.

3. Permanent separation.

6. Request for student biographical sketches. In the onsite classroom, students typically introduce themselves during the first meeting of the class. The introductions are kept brief due to the time constraint on the meeting. Online students have the opportunity to send more descriptive biographical sketches. This ability to have a detailed sharing of one's experience and career history to date is another advantage of the online format. In the onsite classroom, this level of detail in personal history and work would be prohibitive to share since it would be very time consuming. These more complete biographical sketches in the online class can be valuable for the students in getting to know one another and building a class bond, as well as seeing the wonderful diversity of experience, perspectives and work affiliations.

Biographical sketches can be sent to a separate meeting so those students can review them at their leisure. Because of the absence of visual cues, online students tend to be very interested in reading each other's bios. This will also be very helpful to you when making an assessment of class learning needs in preparation of lectures and other course materials.

7. System information, formatting, note and file management. A brief section of the syllabus should be devoted to frequently asked questions as well as system difficulties. Also, if you have preferences regarding limits on student comments or posts to the class, file sizes, or formatting, state this in the syllabus. For example, you may choose to instruct students to briefly excerpt a portion of the note, post or lecture topic that they are responding to and to use subject headings on comments to the class. This section can also clarify your expectations for length of assignments (in terms of the online equivalent of a page) and suggestions for students to follow regarding management of files, including saving all course homework until the final course grade has been received.

Preparing the Online Lecture

Just as the concept of the library with its rows of books and quiet cubicles has changed to include online collections of digital articles and texts, the online classroom is forcing a reassessment of the definition of the lecture. The lecture as an instructional method has been subjected to increasing debate and criticism particularly in regard to its appropriateness for adult learners. Much of the disfavor associated with lectures is that by its very nature, the lecture puts students in a passive role while the instructor remains at the center of attention. The next section of this chapter will examine the role of the lecture in the online medium.

Redefinition of the Lecture

The key to understanding the new possibilities presented in the online lecture will be clearer after distinguishing the environments of the online and onsite classrooms. An understanding of the characteristics of the online environment can enable the online instructor to assess and implement effective techniques to create an exemplary learning experience:

1. Diversity. The online classroom can be distinguished from the onsite classroom by the opportunity it offers for greater differences in the composition of the class. When people think of diversity in the onsite classroom, the focus is more on differences in class composition based on gender, race, physical or learning disability, status, socioeconomic and/or professional status. In contrast, these dimensions of diversity are generally not apparent in the online class. Instead, the online class can be made up of students from around the country or world who would never otherwise be able to assemble together for onsite instruction. This diversity poses a challenge to the instructor to develop a lecture (or lecturette) to meet the needs of a potentially wider range of students in background, experience and expertise.

2. Absence of time pressure for delivery. When an instructor walks into the onsite classroom, he or she is aware of time management responsibility and the need to deliver his or her lecture, review and collect homework assignments, answer questions and leave adequate time for case discussions, class presentations and so on. The clock presents a physical reminder and scorekeeper of the instructor's effort to manage his ort her class effectively. Requests to clarify project requirements, questions about the reading and even the insightful question about course material can end up competing with the time allotted to the lecture. How many onsite lectures have been concluded with, "We are out of time, so read the rest of the chapter and we'll try to get to any questions that you have on it next week."? The class misses out on the complete presentation of the lecture. In the onsite classroom, these factors influence the amount of time that the instructor can give to a lecture as he or she balances varied demands and determine which ones should receive priority for the course period.

The benefits of no time limits on the online lecture presentation are evident in the comments from students, such as the following:

In the traditional classroom, the teacher and students have the allotted time available. With the online lecture, if material is complex, you can take a break and then continue with a fresh mind at a later stage. In the traditional classroom you have to digest the lecture when it is served. This makes the online experience richer than the traditional lecture experience.

I think the online format allows the student to analyze the material at a rate that is more comfortable. With the onsite lectures, the ability to comprehend the subject matter is hampered because of time constraints.

In the absence of a time constraint for the online lecture, how should online instructors decide on the lecture length for their presentations? Some instructors take into consideration the nature of the course itself in determining the length and structure of the lecture. For example, lectures in graduate and qualitative course are somewhat longer than undergraduate and quantitative courses. Many online instructors design a series of lecturettes or mini-lectures to send out over the class week. I prefer the use of mini-lectures that include questions to stimulate discussion on the material. The exception to this is that for courses early in the program sequence, I send out all of the lecture material at the beginning of the week so that less experienced students can see the overall scope of our discussions giving them more time to pace their studies.

Finally, online instructors recognize that the medium requires students to do a great amount of reading and therefore keep their lectures to about 1,500 to 1,800 words. Many students say that the online lecture, unlike the onsite lecture, is never be too long because they don't have to be embarrassed in class for "dozing off." As one student comments, "The lecture is as long or as short as the student's attention span. The student can continue or stop at will." The online environment provides students with the opportunity to truly manage their learning experience.

3. Distractions in the onsite and online class. The environment and the instructor are two examples:

- *The environment.* As an onsite instructor, I would always look forward to presenting lecture material that I had worked on to provide a stimulating and rich learning experience. My preparations and delivery in pursuit of the "flawless lecture" sometimes competed with holding the attention of students distracted by late-arriving classmates, post-dinner dullness and preoccupations with families or jobs that had been left in order to spend the evening in class. For some students, there was the problem of late evening fade-out. I may have been well prepared for the lecture, but the students' mental readiness and the presence of classroom distractions were not fully under my control.

Distractions in the online environment exist for the online student who is attending to a lecture. However, the feedback that I receive from my online students suggests that they utilize the ability they have with online to manage their study time to control distractions as these comments illustrate:

In the onsite lecture, I often found myself missing bits and pieces of the lecture as I attempted to get the main points into my notebook after a long day at work when I was tired. Onsite lectures are also, unfortunately, affected by peripheral considerations that can relate to the physical facility in which the lecture takes place including temperature, seat comfort, those sitting nearby, etc. With the online lecture, none of these peripheral considerations are relevant. There are no facial expressions by the instructor to guide the student's thought one way or another. I can choose the setting and time for reading the lecture. My practice is to review it when I am mentally alert. If I choose, I can read it first thing in the morning and I can review it several times during the week. I can read it over the first time to get the main idea and then again carefully to cull out the main points. I can even cut and paste the lecture into any format I feel comfortable with. With the traditional lecture, when students are overly tired, there is a tendency to 'zone;' unfortunately, they cannot then go to bed and catch it in the morning again when they are fresh. The online lecture gives us that ability.

It is a challenge to juggle professional, family and school responsibilities while also trying to find time for any leisure activities. I tend to live with my portable PC and consequently, I find myself doing schoolwork whenever there's an opportunity. Lately, I have spent a lot of time at airports and on planes, and I will often use this time to read through lectures and other related reading materials. Usually this works fine, but for some work you need peace and quiet. For lectures, I usually get up early before the family is awake.

Online instructors can minimize distractions by writing lectures in a very readable format, presenting full text within a clearly outlined framework. I make my lectures more readable by alternating several different strategies within my presentation of material. These breaks in "pace" are created by designing a "living" lecture—including mini-cases, presenting opposing viewpoints on a subject, debriefing course material, applying course concepts to my own professional experiences, and questioning students to rigorously examine course topics. The purpose of this kind of lecture is to stimulate my students to critically and creatively be involved in the conversation.

- *The instructor.* The quality of the onsite lecture depends on my own delivery and the many factors that will influence that outcome. For example, either my own energy level or the grade dispute that I received moments before I left for class can affect my concentration and thus adversely impact the quality of my delivery of the lecture. In addition, my physical appearance or speaking voice may be a distraction to students, preventing them from becoming more attentive to my otherwise well crafted lecture.

    In the online lecture, visual cues and similar causes of inattention do not exist. In contrast to the onsite lecture, the online lecture's content and delivery are student-focused and become an interactive, discussion between the instructor and the student. The online instructor redirects the student to learn new material, relate course concepts to current professional experiences and become a true partner in the design of the learning experience. In the online lecture, when instructors upload their lectures to the class, each one can potentially deliver that "flawless lecture" irrespective of a long day on a consulting project or a temporary case of laryngitis.

4. Nonverbal Cues. Many instructors enjoy the performance aspect of delivering the onsite classroom lecture. Some of us may enjoy dazzling the class with the drama of the presentation of the historical crisis, using theatrics to make a point. Is there some dramatic equivalent that can be drawn upon in the electronic lecture? Does this drama help promote a student's learning? The following student comments offer evidence that the excitement of the onsite lecture is a real part of the online lecture as well:

Sure, I have had some charismatic onsite lecturers, but I think that the most charismatic ones have been the online ones ;-) really! In a traditional classroom setting, the students are 'forced' to absorb the lecture within a given time period and without any breaks. Consequently, the students will often fall into mental lapses throughout the lectures and the lecturer, therefore, needs to build some 'drama' into the lectures in order to keep the audience awake. This is not the case for online learning where the student can pick the time for studying and can also take breaks or go back and re-read parts of the lecture. Nevertheless, there are many ways for the online lecturer to prove charismatic and add some 'drama.' I think that humor is the most important tool for this.

Quite frankly, I prefer the lack of distracting 'drama' from the instructor. Good novelists can write such artifices into their books; so can online instructors.

Purposes of the Online Lecture

The development of an exemplary online lecture will take into account the unique environment and opportunities of online education as well as the purposes of the lectures and the implications for the role of the online instructor.

Provide Motivation

Given the competency-based orientation of adult learners, it is very important that the online lecture be aligned to the learning preferences of adults. While mastery of the subject material is a primary objective of the lecture, the lecture can also contribute to the learner's motivation to master the subject material. Once instructors have the biographical sketches of their students, they can design the lecture to include material that will appeal to the learning interests of their students.

I stimulate student interest by inserting brief examples or "mini-cases" into my lecture that apply course concepts to their specific industries and problems. By facilitating this linkage of course concepts to students' organizational experiences, students become motivated in this learning process. As one student told me, "I look for an understanding of the material that has been integrated into real life or practical examples and a discussion on the application of the material." This motivation of students to examine real-world application is amplified when the examples discussed are relevant to their own workplaces and experience.

Organize and Prioritize Course Material

The lecture helps to organize and prioritize the material for the week, but the *effective* lecture will do this in a way that involves the student in this process of framing the subject at hand. Rather than writing a lecture that gives solutions and best practices, the lecture can be used as a compass that allows students to select their own direction and question and apply course material to their own experiences and observations. Instead of presenting material as "answers," the lecture can invite students to evaluate the material and raise new questions. The lecture can instruct students to take on a specific workplace problem, examine it in terms of course material and report their findings to the class as part of their participation for the week. For example, course material on organizational structure can be the basis for the students' evaluation of the appropriateness of their own organization's structural designs.

Function as a Technology Conduit

Given the vast resources available to students online, the instructor is in the role of reducing a large amount of information into a manageable number of topics and resources. Online instructors will find themselves "enablers of learning" by acting as a conduit to varied resources based on the learners' needs and interests. The lecture can instruct students to research additional reading material or applications of the topics for the week and to share these resources with the class.

Provide a Model

The instructor's openness and willingness to take some risk through the sharing of professional successes and mistakes can provide a model to students. Online instructors can model other behaviors that are expected in the classroom such as a positive and professional tone, encouraging comments to students, use of humor and critical examination of the material.

Stimulate Critical and Creative Thinking

Use well-placed questions at appropriate points throughout the lecture to invite the students to judge, assess, apply, refute and underscore the impact of what is being accomplished in the presentation. In the onsite classroom where we may feel pressed for time and must move forward through the material to be presented that day, we are not able to give students time to reflect very long on questions, so the potential of this technique may not be fully realized.

In contrast, when the instructor raise the insightful question in the online lecture, students can be invited to take a few minutes to reflect on this, to critique the idea from different viewpoints, to think about how a technique can be used in their own organization or suggest a solution to the problem illustrated in the example just described. We can end the lecture with a "virtual field trip"—an invitation to the students to visit a relevant Internet site. For example, the instructor of a psychology course could send students to an Internet site where they can take a temperament-type test.

Provide a Referral Base for Future Study and Questions

Links embedded in the lecture can break up material with referrals for additional study on the material at hand. Business students can be referred or linked to Internet sites that give examples of the business model just discussed. A music instructor could refer students to Internet sites to compare the music of Mozart and Beethoven. Depending on the technology level of your students, these electronic sidebars can be made optional or specific requirements for the course. The instructor must be aware of changing or unreliable Internet links and select those known for stability. It is a good idea to routinely verify the viability of the links by asking students to bring to your attention any links that are not accessible.

Steps in Developing an Online Lecture

1. Capture and maintain interest. The efficiency of an online lecture saved to a computer file is obvious. One need only retrieve the file and the lecture for the week. But the ongoing improvement and transformation of your online lecture is a process that will make your role as an instructor more interesting and stimulating. The instructor who wants to make learning exciting to students must continue to find teaching itself exciting and challenging. With the ability to modify, update and adapt each lecture to the unique class composition at hand and against a backdrop of changing events, the core lecture can be transformed for each new class. Biographical sketches submitted by students at the beginning of the class can provide the basis for an assessment regarding modification of learning objectives and lectures that are customized to the composition and needs of the group.

In addition, the online instructor will want to identify ways to establish rapport with students who are about to take in the lecture. Onsite instructors can establish rapport with a glance, smile, gesture, or even by walking out among the class members. In contrast, online instructors will convey enthusiasm for the course with the language of the lecture, humor, the sharing of personal and professional examples, and "delivery" style. I have had numerous students tell me that the energy and personality of an online instructor can be effectively communicated "right through the screen."

2. Develop the individual lecture. The lecture will operate on three levels: First, the online lecture efficiently conveys information, theory and subject knowledge to the student. In the absence of real world examples, this level basically offers the student a general formula to apply to the common situation.

The lecture moves to a second level with the your questions about the theory and concepts covered, and the presentation of problems that require students to sort out background facts and issues, apply course material and develop logical alternative courses of action. You can further stimulate students' thinking by adding the third layer which challenges them to test the ideas or techniques discussed—for example, by examining the relationships among specific concepts, applying material to their organization, comparing conflicting points of view or identifying problems, constraints or exceptions.

The difficulty level of the lecture content will typically change over the course because with each week, the students are developing and becoming more experienced learners. Thus, the elements that are used in the first week's lecture cannot become a firm template for the entire course.

3. Prepare the mini-lecture. The onsite class lecture is commonly oriented to the average student in the class in terms of learning interests and background understanding. Questions from students who need additional help or students motivated to discuss more complex topics are handled before or after class and on class break. You can use the mini-lecture to offer comments to meet the specific needs of these two student groups.

Think of the lecture in terms of two components: the core or primary lecture, which is offered on the first day of the class week, and the mini-lecture which is offered as needed on different days over the course. The mini-lecture is a 600- to 800-word lecture that can be used to target additional comments on specific subjects or to reach smaller interest groups within the class. It may happen, for example, that the text focuses on large organizations but the class has several students who are small business owners. In this case, the instructor may want to supplement the primary lecture with mini-lectures that address these learning interests and the concerns that small business owners deal with.

If the class is composed of a cluster of students in one profession or from one industry, such as telecommunications, the online instructor can develop a mini-lecture that applies general course material—for example on managing change—to examples that reflect changes that are taking place in the field of telecommunications. The benefits of the targeted mini-lecture are evidenced in this student's observation:

I have loved the willingness of faculty to offer extra insights in mini-lectures. In my finance class, the text left me baffled, but I found the extra insight from the instructor's targeted lecture extremely helpful.

Conclusion

The online environment offers the exciting possibility for instructors to redefine the nature of the course syllabus and lecture from the traditional teacher-oriented approach to one where the online student becomes actively involved in the learning process. Online instructors can use their syllabi and lectures to engage adult learners in a mental conversation that encourages them to question prior assumptions and challenges their thinking about strategies and current organizational practices. The online syllabus and lecture offer the possibility of a dialogue, an alliance between the instructor and student as partners in the online learning process.

About the Author

Marilyn has a BA from Pomona College in California and an MA and MBA from Cornell University with concentrations in organizational behavior and human resource management. She has 15 years of experience in the field of human resource management, working as a corporate manager, line manager, internal consultant and director of human resources. She has taught for the University of Phoenix for over ten years in the areas of organizational behavior and human resource management. She can be contacted at hrsa@ix.netcom.com.

Chapter 8

ONLINE FACILITATION

Individual and Group Possibilities

by Patricia Addesso

Few things have changed business, education and society as much as the explosive growth of electronic communication. More and more, one hears of virtual teams in the workplace, virtual classrooms in universities and virtual relationships in both business and social contexts. Many professionals are beginning to rethink their basic training and skill base, including medical technicians, psychotherapists and trainers. The world of the instructor must change, as well. How can instructors translate their skills in a way that is useful to the new age of online communication?

It is not difficult to access information these days. Anyone with Internet access has a wide variety of information available to him or her. A traditional teacher who simply provides information can be almost superfluous. But a facilitator is someone who makes learning possible—a role even more important today. This chapter will discuss the art and practice of facilitating learning in the online environment.

Before beginning, a few definitions must be clarified. The *facilitative method* refers to a partnership in which the faculty and students join together to meet learning objectives. The knowledge that each student brings to the classroom is just as important as the knowledge the facilitator brings, and each student learns from fellow students as a result of the facilitated learning discussions. Such facilitation presupposes interactive, group-based learning. The discussion is not about correspondence courses or other one-way teaching methods, nor is the discussion about one-on-one relationships with an instructor.

This chapter refers to learning that is conducted in *asynchronous* fashion. That is to say, students and faculty are not on their computers at the same time, and there is no resemblance to a chat room. People using chat rooms converse in real time. They are all on their computers at the same time, and any message sent by any of the participants in the conversation is seen almost instantaneously. In a message board or newsgroup, a note is posted for all to see. Then the board is checked once or twice a day to see new notes, responses to the original posting, etc. That is what is meant by asynchronous. The facilitator, for example, will post a reading assignment, some comments and a discussion question or two. The students can read the materials, think about the discussion question and respond. They then engage in debate, agreement or argument about the topic(s).

In the sections that follow, I will look at the ways in which online facilitation is similar to traditional facilitation. I will then explore a model of online facilitation, including how to break the ice, how to use specific facilitation skills and how to deal with common problems.

Traditional and Online Facilitation

Facilitating learning in classroom or work groups has a time-honored tradition of basic and advanced skills. Contrary to many people's first impressions, there are many transferable skills between traditional and online facilitation. In fact, in some ways facilitation is more effective online.

Consider the many techniques facilitators have developed to deal with the participant who monopolizes the conversation. In an online discussion, no one is able to speak louder, take up all of the "air time," or dominate due to physical characteristics such as height or attractiveness. Although paying attention to the process is still important, facilitators in the online environment have more opportunity to concentrate on ideas and knowledge.

Traditionally, facilitators also have to pay attention to the nonverbal signals he or she brings to the classroom. In the online environment, it is not possible to judge a participant on regional accent, race, ethnicity or style of dress. This is a huge plus for many people who may not have been "heard" in previous groups due to such differences. Not only the facilitator, but also all of the participants have a "purer" sense of each other as it is unsullied by those preconceived notions.

In the asynchronous environment, there is a distinct separation between *listening* and *talking*. Students "listen" by downloading everything that has been "said" since the last time they logged on. They read the "conversation," paying attention to the pieces that interest them the most. They can then go back over the conversation, pick out the pieces they wish to respond to and do so. There are no lost opportunities to speak or any sense that "I didn't get a turn." In fact, each student may be required to participate as a part of the grade. This process makes it much easier to listen, question and clarify.

The traditional guidelines on facilitation take on fresh life when applied to the new world of online education. In his book *Freedom to Learn*, Carl Rogers (1969) lists the following nine Guidelines for Facilitation. Let's look at each in turn and see how it applies to the online environment.

1. "The facilitator is largely responsible for setting the initial mood or climate of the program."

This is as true online as in the traditional classroom. The facilitator's initial introduction to the course sets the tone as well as the response to each student. For example, an instructor's introduction may include both professional as well as personal information as shown in the following excerpt:

I have a Ph.D. in Industrial Psychology and I am currently an independent consultant operating out of San Diego. My work includes.... On the personal side, I have lived in San Diego all my life (tough job, but someone has to do it!) I have an office in my home where I spend about 60% of my time. I have an 18-year-old cat and a 15-month-old and 17-pound Pomeranian dog.

The instructor may choose the same friendly, casual tone when responding to introductory notes from students. (Note below: "Carat" marks > indicate a quote from a previous message. Also, correspondence examples in this chapter contain fictitious student and company names.) Consider this example:

------In note #35, Joe Smythe wrote:

> I am a Purchasing Manager for a company called Acme. I work at the corporate headquarters in Dallas, Texas and live in a great housing development right near downtown.

>I am single, but engaged to be married to my girlfriend Judith in September.

-----Patricia Addesso replies:

Welcome! We will look forward to your input. What kind of business is Acme in? I get to Dallas a couple of times a year on business—I enjoy the downtown area also, but it's been a little too hot this year! Congratulations on your engagement!

2. "The facilitator helps to elicit and clarify the purposes of the individuals in the class as well as the more general purposes of the group."

Clarifying purposes takes place from the initial communication in the online course introduction and syllabus. Then each individual can express his or her expectations of the course. The question, "What do you hope to gain from this course?" can be answered as part of each students' biographical introductory note.

3. "The facilitator relies upon the desire of each student to implement those purposes which have meaning to him or her as the motivational force behind significant learning."

Assignments, reports and discussions can revolve around implementing the students' goals. If the goal is to apply the course content to the job, for example, online students can be asked specific questions about how a concept or theory applies in the real world.

4. "The facilitator endeavors to organize and make easily available the widest possible range of resources for learning."

The online environment is a great spot for implementing this guideline. At the time he wrote these words, Rogers could not possibly have imagined the resources at one's fingertips in the Internet environment. The key here is to make the resources available and to leave the responsibility in the hands of the students.

When I occasionally ask students to look up an article, some students will ask, "Well, where do I go? How do I find it? Can't you just FAX me the article?" Providing this student with the article does provide her with a resource. But giving some tips on finding it provides a richer resource that can be used again and again.

5. "The facilitator regards himself or herself as a flexible resource to be utilized by the group."

The art of facilitation is best summed up by the word *flexible*. A facilitator knows when to let a conversation go, when to step in and redirect, and when to wrap it up and introduce another topic. A facilitator also decides if and when to interject opinions or facts into the discussion. While the time frames are different, the techniques are the same online. In a classroom, a facilitator may have to wrap up a discussion in 20 minutes, so as to move on to the next agenda item. Even if the class is a smaller, seminar-type group, chances are that not everyone has had a chance to articulate his or her views.

The same online discussion may take several days. In the course of that time, each student may have answered the initial discussion question, responded to classmates' notes and participated in a lively debate. The facilitator decides when to introduce another topic, often simply by observing the tempo of the discussion and noting when it is getting circular or seeming to reach a natural conclusion. The facilitator also chooses the time to introduce his or her own perspective. If, for example, there are a couple of points that he or she considers vital, and those points have not been brought out, the facilitator may interject them. This process is also not all that different from what happens in the traditional classroom.

6. *"As the classroom climate becomes established, the facilitator is increasingly able to become a participant learner, a member of the group, expressing his or her views as an individual."*

Similar to Guideline 5, this one has to do with interjections on the part of the facilitator. The traditional teacher role makes it difficult to express opinions, as the students may be used to taking the teacher's opinions as "law." Communication skills such as uncertainty, labeling opinions and seeking disagreement are very helpful here. For example:

------**Note from Patricia Addesso:**

I think getting employee input into decisions is a critical part of a manager's job. I imagine there are times when it is not appropriate, though. What do you all think?

7. *"The facilitator takes the initiative in sharing himself or herself with the group—feelings as well as thoughts—in ways which neither demand nor impose, but represent simply a personal sharing which the student may take or leave."*

As with Guideline 6, this one requires a certain tentativeness of communication as well as a willingness to expose oneself as a human being. For example:

----Note from Patricia Addesso:

I can certainly remember my first supervisory job. I was 19 and made supervisor of the night shift at a supermarket. I felt amazingly confident, as I look back now. I realize today that I was woefully unprepared both personally and by the organization. My staff included much older specialists in their fields, such as the butchers back in the meat department who would not dream of respecting a 19-year-old female college student. It didn't occur to me to be concerned!

8. "Throughout the course, the facilitator remains alert to expressions indicative of deep or strong feelings."

Deep and strong feelings are present in the online environment, just often a bit subtle and sometimes difficult to "read." A long post from someone who is ordinarily succinct may indicate a strong feeling about something. A "disappearance"—a student who is ordinarily quite participative being quiet all of a sudden—may indicate deep feelings, as well. Of course, it can also mean that the person got busy at work. It needs to be carefully clarified online with the absence of other cues.

In a recent class, we had a discussion on personal values and how they impact decisions. For the first time (four weeks into the class), we discovered that we had an African-American military man in the class, an Asian, and a lesbian. The resulting discussion on personal values became quite heated with the military man telling the lesbian that he was sick of hearing about her homosexuality. Handling such an incident in the traditional classroom would probably have been far more disruptive to the group than this was (see Chapter 10). We all learned something from it; the fact that what is "right" and "wrong" is subjective, and that all of us can be tolerant and accepting right up until our own personal values are challenged.

9. "The facilitator endeavors to recognize and accept his or her own limitations as a facilitator of learning."

As a facilitator, I am not the expert or the final word on a given subject. I can say things like "That's interesting! I never thought about it that way before." I can assign co-facilitators to small group breakout sessions. I can do any number of things that are actually quite freeing; I am under no obligation to have the right answer or to be the ultimate authority.

The preceding examples show that, even though Rogers could not have imagined the online environment as it exists today, his guidelines for effective facilitation still hold up quite well. With these guidelines as our base, the next section will look at a model for online facilitation.

A Model of Online Facilitation

To begin a class, the faculty member may "break the ice," send an introduction to the course and the instructor, and a comprehensive syllabus to the class mailbox. Each student may be instructed to send an introduction and brief biography as well, including information on how much exposure they have had to the topic of the class. For example:

> **Hi all!**
>
> **My name is Elizabeth Grey and I am in my sixth class here. I see a lot of familiar names from Accounting—aren't you glad that's over?**
>
> **For those of you I haven't met, I am a Director of Human Resources for a small company called Futura. We are located in Atlanta, Georgia and I live about 20 miles south of Atlanta in a small community called Elmsville. I have a wonderful husband, two kids (one of each gender) and an OLD OLD cat (she was seventeen last month).**
>
> **I'm looking forward to a change of pace this class. I have been in a lot of the quantitative type courses (Statistics, then Accounting) and Organizational Behavior looks like a breath of fresh air, from what I have seen of the materials.**

Each student and instructor should also have a personal mailbox. That allows for interactions that are inappropriate—for example, assignments turned in, grades or progress reports and some constructive criticisms.

Facilitation Skills

Basic facilitation skills include such things as demonstrating an open and accepting attitude, listening to understand and responding to clarify. Look at how each of these three skills translates to the online environment:

- Demonstrating an open and accepting attitude in traditional classroom may be done through maintaining eye contact, nodding, moving away from the podium or table, appropriate dress and attention to gestures. None of these are a factor online. So how do you demonstrate and open and accepting attitude? Techniques like the use of open questions, use of students' names, reinforcement and encouragement also demonstrate an open and accepting attitude, and all can take place online. For example:

What have the rest of you experienced with this issue?

Jennifer, excellent example, thanks!

- Online facilitators must listen in order to understand the meaning behind student comments. In the online environment, the words used are extremely critical since the nonverbals cannot be seen. One must always ask, never assume (which is a good rule of thumb anyway, of course). For example:

Joe, that last comment about the incident at work sounded a little angry. Were you upset at your boss when you wrote that note?

Often the student's private mailbox is used for such feedback. For example:

Joe, your last exchange with Maria in the class mailbox sounded a bit sarcastic. I don't know if you meant it that way, but maybe saying something like 'I think we can look at it this way' instead of 'It is clearly obvious to anyone who is paying attention...' would come across better. Thanks!

- Online facilitators often respond to clarify meanings. This is done through silence, allowing the speaker enough time to clarify his or her comments, or through summarizing and paraphrasing, and then checking for agreement.

    Sometimes when an online facilitator sees a "strange" comment in the mailbox, silence for a time is helpful. When the student sees his or her own note, he or she will sometimes append a revision, saying something to the effect of "Whoops! That came out wrong." Or a fellow student will ask a clarifying question.

Otherwise, the techniques are the same as those in a traditional classroom. Instead of paraphrasing, the instructor can copy the part of the note that needs clarification, then ask the question. For example:

Re: Note #357 from Russell Jones

I disagree. I have never seen this in my 25 years as a manager.

------reply from Patricia Addesso-------

Hi Russell,

So you have not experienced this phenomenon? That is interesting. Why do you think that is? Remind me, how many different companies have you worked for?

Some of the more advanced facilitation skills also work very well online with just a little revision. Some of the skills include connecting ideas to experience, integrating materials over time, empowering and motivating others, and maintaining a group learning environment. These skills do not require face to face interaction, since they are more oriented to communication skills in general.

Let us take the advanced facilitation skills mentioned above and look at some examples of their use in an online situation. Questions are excellent ways to facilitate adult learning (Bateman, 1990). The following are actual examples of discussion questions used in a master's level organizational behavior course.

Connecting Ideas to Experience
Tell us about a time that you tried to change someone else's behavior at work. What did you do? Did it work? What could you have done differently, using the text or lecture material as a guide?

Integrating Materials over Time
What connections do you see between Margaret's example and the discussion we had last week about cultural diversity in teams?

Empowering and Motivating Others
Thanks for all of the great examples of high-performing teams you have been on. Would anyone care to take a shot at summarizing some of the commonalties between the examples?

Maintaining a Group Learning Environment

Your small group assignment this week is to discuss the case study on pp. 435-437. Identify issues related to organizational behavior that appear in the assigned case study and analyze the issue using the theory from the text or outside research. Identify on page 29 of the textbook which of the areas on the model the issue fits. (For example, is there a communication problem, a motivation problem? How do you know?)

The optimum value will be received from this assignment if you spend much of your energy discussing and analyzing the organizational behavior issue. My hope is that you spend a lot of time in the small group meetings just helping each other understand the issues.

Common Problems

Some of the problems that are familiar to facilitators are *noncontributors, monopolizers, distracters*, and *know-it-alls*. These problems pertain to onsite as well as online classes. Many of the familiar techniques for dealing with them only need to be revised a bit for online, and in fact can work even more effectively. For example, handling a monopolizer in a classroom often means telling him or her, "I'd like someone else to address this question first." Online, that communication can take place in the student's private mailbox, saving them from possible embarrassment.

> **Sharon, I appreciate your enthusiasm and your detailed responses to the discussion questions. My concern is that your classmates are sometimes left with very little to add! Please delay your response a bit, so that others have a chance to think about it. Thanks.**

This problem becomes additionally complicated when the person is a quality contributor. One woman in a class of mine had a tendency to take over discussions and assignments. Far from appreciating it, her classmates resented it. In a private conversation, I likened her behavior to a manager who does not delegate. Since the degree she was pursuing was in management, it was easy to draw some conclusions about how she could use the classroom environment to hone her management and delegation skills, instead of doing all of the work herself.

For the noncontributor (who may just be an introvert) "calling" on them in the classroom is sometimes counterproductive. He or she can become embarrassed and tongue-tied. A personal note online may say:

George, you only made two comments to the main class discussion all last week. Is there a problem or something keeping you busy elsewhere? We'd like to hear more from you this week. Remember, 25% of your grade in this class is based on your participation in the discussion and case study analyses.

Introverts are often more outgoing in the online environment, simply because they have more opportunities to think about their responses and do not have to wait until their turn to talk. Those that are simply less active, however, do need some encouragement. I have had students who felt somehow less qualified to comment on a situation than the others in the class. "I'm just am administrative assistant," said one student. "These other people all seem to have lots of management experience!" Again, the techniques for handling this do not differ at all from what would be done in the traditional classroom. Tell this student how valuable his perspective is and reinforce contributions with, "Good point, John!"

Distracters are familiar to traditional facilitators, as well. They may take the discussion off track, talk about irrelevant issues, or otherwise disrupt the flow of the class. This, too, can again be handled through private communication. Another technique is to create a separate mailbox for socializing, referred to by some online facilitators as the *break room*, the *hallway*, or the *student lounge*. Those students who wish to socialize can do so and those that do not may choose not to "enter" the room.

By now, it should be clear that the last common problem mentioned above, know-it-alls, are handled by way of personal communications and working to diminish the impact on the class. A know-it-all may be sent a message similar to that sent to a monopolizer.

The first time I was preparing to teach a class online, I got a call from one of the students ("Frank") about a week before the class started. Frank introduced himself, we chatted a bit, and then he proceeded to tell me all about another student who was a problem. "We don't like Joe," he said. "He's a know-it-all and hard to get along with. Can you make sure to keep me and my friend Nancy out of any group assignments with Joe?"

Frank and I chatted a bit more, as I checked the roster. Frank's address showed that he was from a mid-sized town in the South, as was his friend Nancy. Joe was from New York City. I decided that I would not take on the responsibility for keeping the feuding parties apart, but would attempt to facilitate a solution.

"Joe has a bad temper," said Frank.

"What did he say or do that led you to conclude that?" I asked.

"We were working on a small group project and Nancy and I had talked about how we wanted to work it. When we told him about it, he got mad and said we obviously didn't care about his input."

"What other interpretations can you think of for his reaction?" I asked. It took some digging, but Frank eventually saw that perhaps Joe was hurt, felt left out, or had even had a bad day at work.

Some issues are specific to the online environment (or are they?) Let's look at two that are commonly mentioned: the "How do I know it is really him?" question and the inability to see nonverbal behavior.

One of the first things many instructors who are unfamiliar with online teaching say is "How do you know your student is who he says he is?" That question, of course, applies in the traditional classroom as well. Few instructors check identification. And in large lecture-type courses, for instance, a student could send a friend in on mid-term day. It is difficult to explain, but people do have online personalities. Without consciously tracking it, an online instructor becomes familiar with a student's tone, word use, and other characteristics. In fact, it is easier to see when a paper may not be a student's original work because every interaction you have with a student is written.

What about the issue of not being able to see nonverbal behavior? First of all, our interpretation of nonverbal behavior is often wrong. Thus, in some cases, there may be actually less misinterpretation online, in some cases. Second, online communication has developed a series of emotional indicators (called *emoticons*) to indicate humor, sarcasm, astonishment, and so on. As one example, if someone makes a statement that is meant to be humorous, they will type in a colon, dash and right parentheses. :-). Looked at sideways, this forms a smiley-face. It is somewhat simplistic, but effective.

Conclusion

If you have ever facilitated learning in a classroom or a boardroom, you already have some of the skills to do so online. The basic guidelines for facilitation, as laid out by Carl Rogers many years ago, provide a fertile common ground for providing the link between traditional and online facilitation. Think of the facilitation process in three parts: (1) the importance of breaking the ice in a positive way, (2) the use of all of the basic and advanced facilitation skills that you have available to you, and (3) the knowledge that problems can be handled and solved. When you break the process down this way, it is clear that there is no mystery about effective online facilitation. The time has come for this new and effective way of teaching and learning.

It is difficult to imagine the changes that will take place in a few short years when it comes to online facilitation. Whether talking about educational institutions, organizational training, or meeting facilitation, everyone must all be prepared to face changes in the way they do business. The critical point here is not to say, "It can't be done," or "It can't be done well," or even "It shouldn't be done." The point is to hone your own skills so that when you are asked to facilitate online, you can transfer our current skills effectively.

References

Bateman, W. (1990). *Open to Ques*tion. San Francisco: Jossey-Bass.

Rogers, C.R. (1969). *Freedom to Learn.* Columbus, OH: Merrill.

About the Author

Patricia is a consultant and trainer in addition to teaching for Jones International University. She has conducted seminars in the Management Development Center of San Diego State University, and was a training and organizational development manager and an organizational development specialist for Cox Communications. She was also the Director of Academic Affairs at San Diego State University. She is the author of *Management Would Be Easy...If It Weren't for the People.* She can be contacted at Paddesso@aol.com.

Chapter 9

KEEPING IT FUN AND RELEVANT

Using Active Online Learning

by Al Badger and Ken White

Active learning is a multi-directional learning experience where learning takes place teacher-to-student, student-to-teacher, and student-to-student. Any form of active learning that is fun or relevant to an online student's professional or personal life tends to motivate the student more than a lecture or discussion on the subject. If learning can be made interesting, the students may learn more. Although online instructors may be eager to get students started on online activities, the successful application of active learning requires coordination and time-management techniques unique to the online environment. This chapter will demonstrate, through a discussion of asynchronicity, pacing and the instructor's role, how active learning can be successfully incorporated in an online course. Sample lesson plans will follow each of the topics of discussion to provide examples of the concepts presented.

Online Learning Activities

Active learning involves activity-based learning experiences: input, process and output. These activity-based experiences can take many forms—whole class involvement, teams, small groups, trios, pairs and individuals—and involve various methods: talking, writing, reading, discussing, debating, and interviewing. Considering the variety of activity-based experiences, active learning is accomplished through innumerable strategies.

Active learning is one of the seven principles established in *Seven Principles of Good Practice in Undergraduate Education* (1987, *AAHE Bulletin)*. In *The Seven Principles in Action*, Susan Rickey Hatfield, editor, David G. Brown and Curtis W. Ellison explain: "Active Learning is not merely a set of activities, but rather an attitude on the part of both students and faculty that makes learning effective. The objective of active learning is to stimulate lifetime habits of thinking to stimulate students to think about HOW as well as

WHAT they are learning and to increasingly take responsibility for their own education." (p 40)

Instructors who use active learning often justify their use with reference to the motivation they provide students. Active learning tends to motivate students. The same holds true for online classroom activities. The online medium is a natural active learning environment as it continues to attract and motivate people who seek information via asynchronous online discussions, game playing and information searches. The medium has become an untamed information source and learning environment for millions. It is a natural choice for many online instructors to choose active learning to get the point across to students.

There are various traditional active learning exercises that translate very well to the online classroom and can be used in conjunction with online lectures:

Questioning
Ask questions in strategic points in the online students' discussion of lecture material. Questions are the simplest form of online interaction that can turn online students into active participants. In addition, you can get a sense of student interest and comprehension.

Pro and Con Listing
Ask online students to list the advantages and disadvantages of any issue raised by text or lecture information. This helps online students to develop analytical and critical thinking skills. When they are encouraged to analyze at least two sides to an issue, they go beyond their initial reactions.

Brainstorming
Ask online students to generate ideas and record them without evaluation or judgment. This process promotes participation from all students because they do not have to worry about their ideas being rejected. Online students learn to save critiquing of ideas until after all ideas have been listed and acknowledged.

Formative Quizzes
Ask online students collectively to respond to formative quizzes that are used simply for the sake of learning. Participation is increased as online students reach consensus about correct responses. This also allows online instructors to gain information about how familiar students are with course concepts.

Dyads

Ask online students to pair up and discuss questions or ideas. After students discuss the question or idea with their partner, they can share their results in a large class discussion. In dyads, many online students are more willing to share their ideas. It also forces participation by students who might not otherwise do so in larger groups.

Debates

Ask online students to form two groups to debate opposite sides of an issue. You can arbitrarily divide students evenly on two sides of an issue. Have each group work separately to develop an assigned position and to create a course of action. The two groups can then meet in a common forum and follow a traditional debate format.

Conducting online class activities is not easy. To help explore these techniques and minimize this challenge, we will now explore barriers to successful online activities and demonstrate how active learning can be successfully incorporated in an online course. We will first consider the issues of *asynchronicity, visibility, pacing and the instructor's role.*

Asynchronous Online Activities

When we first heard the word *asynchronous* many years ago, we had no idea what it meant. Peers and colleagues would bandy the word about in online discussions while I pretended to understand. After a short time of working online, though, it started to make. It simply meant that online students and instructors do not have to be at one place at one time to participate in a class activity. It continues to be the heart and soul of online communication and learning within many educational institutions.

Asynchronous learning networks eliminate the instructional impediments of space and time while providing a degree of student-faculty interaction and collaboration that is truly unique. Schedules become flexible and no one needs to wait for others before attending a class. Particular rhythms of online communication are set, and discussion flow and class rapport are established. Better yet, student responses are allowed considerable time for reflection before being sent. The quality of interaction and dialogue can be enhanced.

On the other hand, the asynchronous mode has a down side and that is mostly related to the delay in response time. When online students ask a question or respond to each other, they often have to wait a full day to get a response. When you add to this mix of eight to thirteen students in one class sending and responding to each other, a response to a message, comment or question can be as long as two days. This time delay can be a problem when it comes to running online group activities. Just getting thirteen people in an asynchronous online classroom to discuss and agree on a concept can take a week. Consequently, the first lesson for an online instructor in an asynchronous online environment is: *When dealing with delayed response time, gauge the length of the activity carefully.*

Although online asynchronous learning activities may take longer to conduct, instructors can run various activities simultaneously in different online group meetings. For example, Al creates one forum or meeting in which students are involved in an activity like *Lifeboat.* At the same time in another meeting, a case study discussion is well on its way. In yet another meeting, online students are sharing and editing each other's research reports. Limits, of course, exist for this strategy, but running simultaneous online activities in this way works more smoothly when students need not be in one scheduled location at a specific time.

In addition, methods exist to handle the frustrations inherent to delayed response time. Delayed response time can tend to scatter the focus of an online activity, so keeping the students focused on the activity is important. The second lesson for the online instructor, then, is: *Ask open-ended questions during each day of the activity to help remind the students that you are watching the direction of the activity.* Even asking controversial questions during such activities may motivate the online student to take a position whereas if you did not, he or she might remain uninvolved.

That said, and remembering the importance of gauging time and being visible, the following activity works particularly well in an asynchronous mode. Especially note how the days are scheduled so that the asynchronous nature of online is taken into full consideration.

Virtual Field Trip Online Activity

Virtual field trips continue to grow in popularity. On a virtual field trip, you can take your online students just about anywhere—there are thousands of virtual field trips online students can take. The experience is an excellent model of an online teaching strategy that was not possible before the advent of computers in education. Virtual field trips benefit online students and instructors, giving online instructors the chance to stretch old paradigms about how to teach and online students the chance to try active approaches to learning.

Finding accurate answers to questions is a valuable learning skill. The virtual field trip described in this section exposes online students to a variety of online references—including websites, databases, and other online resources. It offers differentiated activity choices and emphasis is placed on search strategies rather than specific individual resources. It can help new online students develop some online searching strategies and learn how to find information using web sites, databases, and other online resources.

Outcome

Online students who complete this virtual field trip will accomplish several learning outcomes, including accessing remote information, using web environments, evaluating the accuracy and relevance of electronic information and participating effectively in groups to pursue and generate information. The search strategies involved in navigating this virtual field trip will also require critical thinking, observation and categorization, and teamwork.

Process

This lesson will probably take a week online. It can be taught all in one day in a synchronous online learning environment, but it will more than likely take place over the course of six to seven days in an asynchronous situation. The field trip is multi-disciplinary, in that web resources from several subject areas will be covered. Online students will be paired with one another student for this experience. Ideally, these students can choose a compatible path for their trip. All of the resources necessary for navigating this learning experience are included in the field trip, so it should be easy enough for a novice online instructor to use.

Procedures

The procedures of this lesson are as follows:

(1) On Day 1, upload a lecture where you introduce the websites for the virtual field trip, identify the outcomes of the learning experience so that the online students understand the purpose of the activity, and offer tips on critically assessing information online.

(2) Provide the students with a travel agenda and timetable for visiting the places in the itinerary.

(3) Pair up students and assign their specific web site(s). Each member of a team should be assigned different tasks. It is useful to assign students unique websites and tasks that may overlap slightly so that when they report their

progress on Day 3, some information will be similar for verification purposes, while other information is unique to a particular pair of students and to a particular student in a pair. For example, you could assign websites for presidential candidates or various environmental groups. One student could look at the accuracy of the information while the other could look at issues of relevancy.

(4) Give your students clear deadlines of what should be accomplished by what day.

(5) On Day 3, students should send the results of the first phase of their field trip to the main class forum—what website they visited, a description of the website and the kind of information it offers, and an evaluation of the accuracy and relevance of the website's information. Show your involvement and challenge students to go beyond their initial reactions. Ask questions and encourage the students to question each other's data.

(6) On Day 4, prepare students for the final phase of their field trip that will be due on Day 6. The lesson will conclude on Day 6 with students providing a three-paragraph summary of their virtual field trip.

(7) On day 6, students post their three-paragraph summaries where they describe what they learned, the advantages and disadvantages of going on a virtual field trip rather than visiting in person and the pros and cons of online teamwork.

Closing and Follow-up
This virtual field trip should help online students to develop searching strategies that they can use to locate information when they are using various online resources throughout their educational experience. As follow-up activities, We discuss with students what worked and what did not and survey my students for information about refining this active learning for the future. We look for feedback about issues of asynchronicity.

The Importance of Visibility and Pacing

Daily participation is important for both the online instructor and the online student. Effective online communication and learning depend on *visibility*. New online instructors tend to underestimate the importance of visibility for maintaining a sense of presence. Traditional instructors are accustomed to wandering about the classroom during group discussions while listening in on each group. In an onsite classroom, students are quite aware of the instructor's presence and even increase the involvement level of their discussion as the instructor nears their group. An instructor can also use body language to motivate or communicate an idea to the class. Thus a traditional onsite instructor can influence and even direct the students' learning just by his or her physical presence in the classroom. Instructors can take this aspect of physical presence for granted until they begin teaching online.

If an online instructor does not compensate for this hidden aspect on physical presence, students are quick to let him or her know. The concern begins with public questions to other online students in their class such, "Where is the instructor?" Within days of this first observation, students feel abandoned, even though the instructor may have been reading the online class discussion on a daily basis. When it comes to visibility and instructional participation, there is a third rule for the online instructor: *If you are not participating (i.e., providing input to the class) and talking in this asynchronous classroom, you are not there. Out of sight is out of mind.*

Does this mean that online instructor should send notes to the classroom every day? Let us answer this question with advice we each often give students who are new to asynchronous, online education. We offer the same advice to new online instructors:

The real challenge in the online classroom is managing one's time effectively. I have a technique that helps me manage time online and it may work for you. The way I like to organize my online time is by logging on daily. How does this allow me to manage my online time better? Well, if I wait a few days to logon, my mail box collects so many notes and the discussion forums get filled with so many comments that it can take hours for me in one sitting to read through them and respond. It becomes a major task that can interfere with my whole and one that I do not look forward to. I do not know about you, but I do not have three or fours hours in a day to read through and respond to all my notes. However, I do have one to two hours each day for online interaction. I find that I can manage my online time best by logging on each day. When I logon daily, I spend one to two hours responding to messages. Since my daily schedule can handle one to two hours of online time, I feel more in control of how I manage time. If I pace myself and logon everyday, even for a short time, I better manage my time and the online work that I need to do. And in addition, I enjoy the experience more!

Students respond very positively to this message because they begin to experience the special circumstances of the asynchronous, online learning environment and accept the practical need to logon daily and save time.

While visibility is the salt, *pacing* is the pepper to facilitating an effective online learning activity. When preparing for an online activity, an instructor should set up clear expectations of participation and pacing through a daily schedule. Inform the students, for example, that on Day Two they are expected to send the results of an assigned task to the class forum. On Day Four, they are to respond to tasks A and B, etc. A fourth rule for the online instructor is: *Clear expectations about participation will help make students accountable for visibility and pacing.* Expectations and procedures remind both the students and you to contribute and to pace yourselves. Planning to send a particular question or more information during Day Three of an activity or discussion, for instance, not only helps the discussion to evolve but also adds consistency to how the class is taught. Together, they are efficient ways to keep the pacing of the class moving.

The following sample online activity shows how an instructor can manage the pacing of an online class. Pay close attention to how many days occurs between one set of assignments and another.

Information Scavenger Hunt Online Activity

This active learning exercise involves a scavenger hunt for web sites relevant to the course content. Scavenger hunts have become a popular tool for teaching online students how to access and use the resources and information available on the Internet. There are many reasons for the growing popularity. Among them:

- Online scavenger hunts are easy to create and interactive searches are both fun and informative for students.
- Online scavenger hunts can be adapted to virtually any curriculum area, simultaneously providing online students with technological and subject matter knowledge.
- Online scavenger hunts can be a whole class activity, a team activity, or a review or challenge activity for individual students.
- Online scavenger hunts can be as simple or involved as the learning objectives dictate. New online students may be provided with only a few questions, along with the links or URLs necessary for finding the answers, while experienced online students may be given a broad topic and asked to find their own sources for obtaining necessary information.

Each student is given a set of questions related to a specific course topic. Online students then explore the university or college's online library to answer the questions.

Outcomes

This activity will provide students the opportunity to navigate through various websites, to become familiar with the various search engines available on the Internet and to understand the limitations to Internet searches.

Process

This lesson will probably take four or five days online. The scavenger hunt is multi-disciplinary, in that web resources from several subject areas will be covered. Online students can hunt individually or students can form groups for this experience. The activity can also be competitive. As the instructor, you can award points based on what individual or team submits the first answers and who gets the most correct answers for their topic. Again, all of the resources necessary for navigating this learning experience are included in the scavenger hunt, so it should be easy enough for a novice online instructor to use.

Procedures

The procedures of this lesson are as follows:

(1) On Day One, provide a lecture that introduces some main search engines available on the Internet, gives them a topic for research and assigns students the task of answering twenty questions about that topic. The answers to these questions can be found on websites that students discover through the search engines. (A version of this activity asks students to use the search engines introduced in the lecture to locate the answers to ten of the questions. The other ten must be found on search engines and websites that students have discovered on their own.)

(2) On Day Two, make sure that students understand that they will identify where they found the answers to the questions. This requires that students list the web address where the information was located. All websites must be verifiable.

(3) By Day Three, have students send the answers to their scavenger hunt questions to you or the main class forum. You will need the answers in order to determine who submitted them first and to correct the answers. But it is also

valuable for the whole class to see the answers to the questions as it informs them about various topics beyond their own.

(4) On Day Four, prepare students for the final assignment of their online scavenger hunt that will be due on Day Five. The lesson will conclude on that day with students providing a three-paragraph summary of their scavenger hunt.

(5) Have students post their three-paragraph summaries where they describe what they learned, the advantages and disadvantages of various search engines and the pros and cons of using the Internet as a research tool rather than the traditional library.

Closing and Follow-up

This online scavenger hunt should help online students to develop searching strategies that they can use to locate information when they are using various online resources throughout their educational experience. This activity can continue to Day Six where you can pose follow-up questions and generate a final discussion. For example, you can ask: *"What has been the most challenging aspect of this exercise and how have you solved this challenge?"* or *"What are some of the techniques and tools that you discovered so far?"* Conclude the discussion and the activity with tips and tools that will help the students navigate the Internet. As possible follow-up, we discuss with students what worked and what did not and survey my students for information about refining this active learning for the future. We look for feedback about issues of pacing.

The Role of the Instructor

The role an instructor takes during any online learning activity will depend on the objectives of that activity. Some activities may be conducive to allowing the instructor to join as an equal participant while others may not. Being an instructor who participates in an activity is yet another way to keep students on track and involved. Participation allows the instructor to model the behavior that one would like the students to follow. Al often set himself up as the point of attack during an online activity. For example, he might take a position that is obviously controversial to force students to take and defend a position. Although this technique is not exclusive to online activities, it is equally successful in an online class. Taking such a position in an online learning activity also affords the instructor the opportunity to redirect the ideas without dominating the discussion. Students often take up discussing non-related topics. An instructor can ask a leading question to force discussion of the content.

The potential downside of an instructor's participation is the possibility of the instructor's dominating the group discussion. Online learning is best as a facilitated experience rather than a place for an instructor's diatribe, so the effective online instructor often wants to avoid becoming center to any group activity. Another drawback to instructional participation is that it often attracts students who want to tell an instructor what he or she wants to hear. Consequently, a fifth rule for online instructors is: *If an instructor's participation in an activity is too much or too little, the learning environment tends to get polluted and an instructor often finds him- or herself not knowing what the students are really thinking or learning from the experience.*

The instructor's decision whether or not to participate in an online activity depends on the following:

- *The type of activity.* If the exercise requires no specialized knowledge, instructor participation as an equal player does not conflict with the facilitating pedagogy. If, however, the instructor is the expert, it does interfere.
- *The type of online student.* If the student is less experienced online, then the instructor might choose to guide rather than participate. If, however, the student is experienced online, then the instructor as an equal participant would be welcomed.

The following online activity is perfect for instructional participation. Online students love it when the instructor gets thrown out of the starship by the end of the exercise. Students tell us that they get more out of the activity than they do without us.

Space Colonists Exercise Online Activity

The following exercise is organized for an asynchronous online classroom that runs for seven days. As the instructor, you should participate as one of the players in this exercise, using it as an opportunity to provide direction or blatant examples of logical fallacies. If the class is large, small groups of eight can be created. Students can then be split into smaller class meetings where they can conduct the debate. On Day Six, each group can select a leader to present the results and the rationale for each group's decision.

Outcomes

This exercise will provide online students the opportunity to argue logically, identify logical fallacies in arguments, understand how generalizations and stereotypes can influence reasoning and demonstrate how cultural norms influence perceptions.

Process

This exercise is derived from the well-known game called *Life Boat* or *Bomb Shelter.* Online students play assigned characters who are space colonists on a starship on its way to a new world. The starship is designed to sustain nine to eleven colonists for five years, the duration of the trip to the new world. Unfortunately, a meteor has struck the starship and damaged it, so there is now only enough oxygen for five colonists for the five-year period. As a result, the colonists must decide which five should stay and which should go.

Procedures

The procedures for this lesson are as follows:

(1) On Day One, send a lecture on logical fallacies to the online class. The lecture should focus on how one can determine whether or not an argument is a good one. For example, in analyzing readings, how can online students know whether or not an author has made a strong argument? What do they look for? The lecture should explain how *fallacious reasoning*—faulty induction or deduction—can undermine an argument, and give examples of fallacies that have been identified and labeled. You can get a full list of fallacies at http://www.don-lindsay-archive.org/skeptic/arguments.html but here are some of the most common fallacies:

- **Hasty Generalization**: A generalization accepted on the support of a sample that is too small or biased to warrant it. Example: *All welfare recipients are lazy.*
- **Post Hoc Ergo Procter Hoc:** A hasty generalization in which it is inferred that because one event followed another, it is necessarily caused by that event. Example: *The rooster crowed and then the sun rose. Therefore, the rooster caused the sun to rise.*
- **Non Sequitur:** A premise has no direct relationship to the conclusion. This fallacy often appears in political speeches and advertising. Example: *In a commercial, a waterfall in the background and a*

beautiful woman in the foreground have nothing to do with an automobile's performance.

- **Begging the Question:** A circular argument where a conclusion is assumed to be true in order for the premise to be accepted. Example: *I deserve an "A" because I am an "A" student.*
- **Contrary of Fact Hypothesis:** An argument that depends on an event that did not happen. Example: *If I had married Bob, I would be happy today.*
- **Ignoring the Question:** An argument that shifts from one subject to another in order to appeal to an emotional attitude that has nothing to do with the logic of the case. Example: *National health care is socialized medicine.*
- **False Analogy:** An unsound form of an inductive argument where the argument is based completely on analogy to prove its point. *Example: This is a great car because, like the finest watches in the world, it was made in Switzerland.*
- **Either/or Thinking:** This fallacy assumes that a choice is between two opposite extremes instead of allowing for a middle alternative. Example: *You are either for us or against us.*
- **Common Belief:** The fallacy where a statement is believed to be true or false on the evidence that many other people believe it or do not believe. Example: *Darwin's theory of evolution cannot be true because most Americans do not believe in it.*
- **Past Belief:** The claim for belief is supported by belief in the past. Example: *There must be life after death because the ancient Egyptians prepared for an afterlife.*
- **Attacking the Person:** This fallacy attacks the person rather than the position. Example: *The environmentalist's ideas on global warming cannot be true because he lives in a big house.*
- **Appeal to Authority:** An argument that appeals to an expert in one field but on a topic not within that field. Example: *The physicist does not believe in god, so god must not exist.*
- **Bandwagon:** This fallacy appeals to emotions and asks the listener to join a crowd of believers. Example: *Everybody speeds, so it is OK.*
- **Red Herring:** This fallacy introduces an irrelevant issue into the discussion as a diversionary tactic. Example: *The death penalty deters crime because it is payback for the victim's family.*
- **Questionable Cause:** A cause for an occurrence is identified without sufficient evidence. Example: *The car in front of us is swerving side to side, so the guy must be drunk.*

- **Straw Man:** This fallacy misrepresents an opponent's position in order to attack it. Example: *If we regulate guns, only criminals will have guns.*

- **Appeal to Ignorance:** This argues that something must be true because it has not been proven false. Example*: I believe in UFOs because no one has proven to me that they do not exist.*

- **Two Wrongs Make a Right:** Justifying an apparently wrong action by charges of another wrong action. Example: *The instructor did not explain the concepts well enough, so it is OK to cheat.*

- **Amphibole:** A premise is ambiguous because of careless or ungrammatical phrasing. Example: *Last night I caught a prowler in my pajamas.*

- **Equivocation:** The arguer uses the ambiguous language to make a reason appear more convincing. Example*: The sign said "fine for parking here", and since it was fine, I parked there.*

- **Appeal to Emotion:** The arguer uses emotional appeal rather than logical reason to persuade the listener. Example: *Aren't you afraid that you will go to hell if you don't tell the truth?*

Include the following statement in the lecture:

You are space colonists on the way to populate a new world. You are the sole survivors of the human race as a major catastrophe destroyed Earth. Your starship was designed to sustain nine to eleven colonists for five years, the duration of the trip to the new world. Unfortunately, a meteor has struck the starship and damaged it. You now have only enough oxygen for five colonists for a five-year period. As a result, the colonists must decide which five should stay and which should go.

You will each be assigned a character to play on Day One. Each character will have a special background. It is important that you introduce your assigned character to your group before Day Two. Provide full disclosure of your character's background. You may embellish somewhat, but you cannot change the nature of the character's story. After all the students have introduced themselves as their characters, the group must decide who should stay and who is to go. The discussion for this decision should begin by Day Three. Remember, one goal is to repopulate the new world so you should keep this in mind when you are deciding. It is important to note that suicide is not permitted and you cannot volunteer to leave the spacecraft.

(2) Assign the characters on Day One. Allow the students one to two days to prepare reasons why they should stay in the starship.

(3) Instruct the students to note logical fallacies as they listen to each other's arguments and counter arguments. A class discussion on fallacies that surface during the exercise will follow on Day Six and Seven.   Below is a list of characters for this exercise (you can make-up more if you need them). Assign characters randomly and include yourself. For example, you might write each character on a slip of paper, put them in a box and draw one character for each student on your roster. Then tell the students:

This is your character and story. Introduce your character and present the information in a persuasive form. The information below is basic and you may embellish as long as you don't change the character's background.

PROFESSION: Medical Doctor
AGE: 63
GENDER: Female
STORY: **You have an unusual memory problem. There are days when you don't know who or where you are.**

PROFESSION: Radiation Expert
AGE: 44
GENDER: Male
STORY: *You have had a violent past and are capable of hurting people.*

PROFESSION: Prostitute
AGE: 28
GENDER: Male
STORY: *You have a photographic memory. You remember every client.*

PROFESSION: Nurse
AGE: 27
GENDER: Female
STORY: *You have terminal cancer and could die at any time.*

PROFESSION: Lawyer
AGE: 30
GENDER: Male

STORY: *You are an ambulance chaser, and untrustworthy, but you also have an excellent sense of logic.*

PROFESSION: Pilot
AGE: 38
GENDER: Female
STORY: *You were drunk and flying over some part of Russia. Being too intoxicated to think straight, you pressed a button on the plane that dropped four nuclear bombs. Because of this accident, America and Russia went to war.. The result, of course, is a nuclear war that placed you all in this starship.*

PROFESSION: Police Officer
AGE: 27
GENDER: Male
STORY: *You have delayed stress syndrome from a past incident and you now often freeze when danger is near.*

PROFESSION: President of the United States of America
AGE: 49
GENDER: Female
STORY: *You are a strong proponent of women's right and worked hard to make opportunities available to women in traditionally male-oriented jobs. In fact, you have a bias that women can do things better than men.*

PROFESSION: Psychiatrist
AGE: 38
GENDER: Male
STORY: *You tend to psychoanalyze everyone to the point that you have never had a social life. You also tend to write yourself prescription drugs for recreational use. The drugs fried your brain but you have moments of extreme brilliance and creativity.*

PROFESSION: Soldier
AGE: 29
GENDER: Male
STORY: *You are a recovered addict and while you have excellent marksman skills, you have major trouble with the stress of human relationships. You fly because you like to be alone on the cockpit.*

PROFESSION: University Student
AGE: 19
GENDER: Female
STORY: *You are four months pregnant. You are also a psychic and believe that your child is the new savior.*

PROFESSION: Survival Expert
AGE: 29
GENDER: Male
STORY: *When you were younger, you were very concerned about the world's overpopulation problem. In order to do your part and not add to this growing population, you had an operation that now prevents you from fathering children.*

PROFESSION: Teacher
AGE: 38
GENDER: Female
STORY: *Like the Survival Expert, you cannot have children. You taught at an elementary school back on Earth.*

(4) Give students five days to complete this exercise. Explain the time limit and that a decision must be made before the end of Day Five.

(5) Send a reminder at the end of Day Five that once the aspects of the decision have been explored, the class will discuss the types of fallacies that surfaced during the exercise.

(6) On Day Six, tabulate and compare results. Invite discussion as to what social or cultural factors were at play in influencing decisions. For example, were some professions considered bad because of logical fallacies?

(7) On Day Seven, ask students to explain why certain fallacies may have been more convenient to use than others. Explore how some of these fallacies might be tied to cultural, economic, sexual and political perceptions and norms. Finally, have students collectively list the fallacies that they observed.

Closing and Follow-up

Conclude the lesson by emphasizing the source of fallacies and summarize how perceptions influence the way people evaluate information and other people. As possible follow-up, we discuss with students what worked and what did not and survey students for information about refining this active learning for the future. We look particularly for feedback about the role of the instructor.

Conclusion

Learning activities can be very successful in an online classroom. The asynchronous learning environment involves designing activities with time delays in the communication flow in mind. This chapter attempted to provide online instructors with some examples of successful online activities. As an online educator, you must understand the asynchronous nature of online communication. You must also provide students with a daily schedule of events to help them with pacing, and successfully move students through each step of the activity. And you need to appreciate that online communication and learning depend on visibility, both for students and instructors. Finally, you must always decide if it would be better for you to participate as an equal participant or as an observer of the activity. If you take into consideration all the issues presented in this chapter, you will be well on your way to designing and conducting a successful online activity.

References

Chickering, A.W, and Gamson, Z.F. (1987). Seven Principles for Good Practice in Undergraduate Education. *AAHE Bulletin*, 39 (7), 3-7.

Hatfield, S.R. (1995). *The Seven Principles in Action.* Anker Publishing Company: Bolton, MA.

Kahane, H. (1992). *Logic and Contemporary Rhetoric: The Use of Reason in Everyday Life.* Belmont, CA: Wadsworth Publishing Company.

Reid, J.M. (1988). *The Process of Composition.* New York: Prentice Hall, Inc.

Seech, Z. (2004). *Open Minds and Everyday Reasoning.* Belmont, CA: Wadsworth Publishing Company.

About the Author

Al received his M.A. in education from Ohio State University. Former Director of Student Services at the University of Phoenix Online, Al is also the creator of a cartoon strip called "Phritzy's World."

Chapter 10

DEALING WITH CHALLENGING SITUATIONS

Communicating Through Online Conflict

by Ken White

Some level of frustration and controversy is normal fare for faculty and students in the online learning environment. Online faculty often encounter difficult students who may dominate a class discussion, challenge course content, resent the authority or expertise of the instructor, display rude and inappropriate tone to other class members, refuse to adhere to the class structure and an assignment schedule, or simply not participate. In addition, if conflicts are bad enough and are ignored long enough, the results can end up in the hands of administrators or even in a nasty lawsuit. The real task at hand is responding effectively to online conflicts before they get to the point where deans or attorneys are called in.

Although disagreement and conflict are inevitable aspects of all human relationships, the need to respond effectively in online conflict situations is particularly important. Sproull and Kiesler (1991) have shown that people interacting on computers are isolated from social cues and feel safe from surveillance and criticism. As a consequence of the low level of nonverbal and social information available online, messages are often startlingly blunt and discussions can easily escalate into name-calling and other forms of abusive and contemptuous behavior. Such "flaming" messages do not go unnoticed and can be met with numerous reactions that even resort to stronger language. Before the online instructor is even aware of a "flame war," the social fabric and learning climate of the class can be severely damaged.

Consequently, it is understandable if new online faculty members accept the long held view that conflict is inherently negative and try to stay away from it. The fact that some online "talk" becomes more extreme and impulsive can be seen as revealing a weakness in the medium, a flaw in its design, operation and communication processes. In an environment where students feel less bound by convention and less concerned with consequences, conflict can be seen as something to be avoided. Sources of conflict have to be identified and eliminated as soon as possible. Peace and stability have to be returned to the online classroom

The view of online conflict in this chapter is quite different. I want to emphasize that online conflicts are neither inherently negative nor positive. It's what we make of them. The focus of this chapter is on helping online teachers respond effectively to online conflict.

As a preface, I make a distinction between *reacting* and *responding*. I associate reactive behavior with the concept of *movement*. It's like a physical process we find in nature. Like movement, reacting is reflexive—it is fight or flight. On the other hand, I consider responsive behavior more like the concept of *action*. It is a human practice involving thinking and choice. That is, responding is reflective. Unlike reptiles that react, humans are able to respond.

Online conflict is responded effectively to (or not) through communication. As I will discuss later in this chapter, if one "reacts," to conflict, one ignores or cancels out one or more of the crucial communication elements of conflict. By recognizing those communication elements, one can eliminate *reactive* or ineffective ways of communicating through online conflict and begin to *respond* effectively. One can benefit from reflecting on our own attitudes about conflict and on our own communication skills, because while all online conflict is not rooted in poor communication, it always involves communication.

The starting point for responding effectively to online conflict is to ask yourself what it is you want to have happen. Focus on what is positive, specific and practical. To begin, online conflicts can be responded to effectively by looking at three key areas: (1) What is online conflict and how does it work, including its benefits? (2) What are the different types of online conflict? and (3) What can online faculty and students do about each type?

Online Conflict as Communication

A few years ago, the American Management Association sponsored a survey of managerial interests in the area of conflict. The respondents in the survey were 116 chief executives, 76 vice presidents and 66 middle managers. These executives and managers revealed what they considered to be the principle causes of conflict. Among the described causes were:

- Communication failure
- Personality clashes

- Value and goal differences
- Substandard performances
- Responsibility issues

Two important lessons for online teaching and learning can be drawn from the study. First, there are many grounds for conflict and they are not limited to onsite situations. Whenever people are involved in interdependent and interactive relationships, such as the virtual or online organization, there are many situations over which conflicts can arise. Second, it may be quite challenging to get a handle on the complex and often subjective dynamics of conflict, particularly in the electronic classroom.

Consequently, the initial step responding effectively to conflict situations is to know what the conflict is about and how it works. Once you have made some sense out of conflict and its communication dynamics, you are better able to figure out what you can do about it. I want to offer a communication-oriented definition of *conflict* that suggests specific ways for communicating through online conflict situations.

I agree with John Stewart when he defines *conflict* as communication—verbally and nonverbally expressed disagreement between individuals or groups. Though broad, Stewart, Zediker and Witteborn's (2007) definition says several particular things about conflict. First, conflict is expressed with words or through nonverbal behaviors such as communication tone, which is an important factor in online communication. Sometimes, online students use words to express their disagreement by writing, "I disagree with what you are saying!" At other times, it is the lack of words and participation that clearly signal disagreement.

Second, when seen as communication, conflict is *expressed,* as opposed to feelings that happen inside a person. The definition concentrates on communication, not on psychology. It does not encourage one to speculate about or interpret the motives of the person on the other end of the computer, but to focus on how both people communicate. It is a reminder that conflict is always about a relationship between two or more people.

Third, and most importantly, Stewart's definition emphasizes that conflict is a natural part of human interaction. Conflict is essentially about different points of views. People have disagreements because they are different. Because they are not the same, and because they see and value things differently, people vary in their beliefs as to what things are or should be. Although conflict may divert time and energy away from tasks, represent the various issues that polarize individuals and groups within organizations, and obstruct cooperative action and decreases productivity, it is also a creative and positive force. It is important to recognize that, as communication, online conflict has some benefits.

Benefits of Online Conflict

If online conflict is inevitable and natural—if it represents the uniqueness of all people—then it is not always negative. If a major part of the problem about responding effectively with online conflict is one's tendency to think only about the negative part of it, then one needs to "mutate your metaphors" about conflict. People can begin to see the benefits of online conflict.

The list of positive and creative values inherent in online conflict is equally long. Conflict has the potential to do the following:

- Open up hidden issues
- Clarify subject-matter
- Improve the quality of problem-solving
- Increase involvement in learning
- Increase cooperation and interaction

Online conflicts can be valuable and productive both for faculty and students. For the online instructor, conflict can stimulate creative problem solving, generate more effective ideas and fine-tune learning relationships. For online students, conflict can provide opportunities to test, expand and demonstrate skills; to better understand their co-learners; and to develop confidence and trust. Specifically, conflicts can help to do the following:

1. *Develop more interpersonal online relationships.* There is a potential for human understanding that a legitimate disagreement can bring to the online classroom. Conflict can help people learn something new about each other and remind them of each other's humanity. One can develop understanding that goes beyond the subject matter of what one is learning to an appreciation of who one is. For example, say that there is a hidden conflict in an online ethics class about some students imposing their religious beliefs on others. In a discussion about the range of ethical theories, "Richard" declares that Christianity is the only true ethical viewpoint. He shares his Christian beliefs in every note he sends to the class discussion. He shows no sensitivity to other perspectives. Another student, "John," expresses no concern in the class, but

eventually sends the instructor a personal message and writes in no uncertain terms, "If you don't stop this guy, I'm going to give him hell!"

The online instructor could avoid the possible benefit of conflict in this situation by ordering the class as a whole to respect all opinions and not to share their personal moral views. Instead, the instructor sends Richard a personal message and poses the problem to him. He describes the feeling and frustrations of the other students as well as one student's reluctance to join in the discussion, and asks how the situation should be handled. In response, Richard writes back that he does have strong beliefs, that he was not aware of the feelings of the other students, and that he will try to be less pushy. The instructor then supplements his communication with a telephone call to Richard, thanking him for his productive response and talking in more general terms about how the class is going, what the weather is like in Richard's hometown, and sharing personal information about jobs and family.

This example shows how online students often lack tangible reminders of their audience. Lacking the paralinguistic resources to help him convey his ideas, Richard resorted to even stronger language to express his passion of belief. Without a face to remind him of his audience and to temper his words, Richard forgot about convention and consequences. He needed to be reminded of the interpersonal element without increasing a sense of isolation that is common online. The instructor accomplished this by focusing on Richard's humanity, as well. Consequently, one result of the conflict was about tasks and relationships: a working relationship was formed. But a second result was even more important: Richard realized that he did not handle the interpersonal part of the online conflict very well—he did not remind himself of the person on the other end of the computer. The conflict taught him that he was "talking with" other people online who have feelings, thoughts and lives of their own.

2. *Promote workable decisions in the online class.* The adversary system of the country's courts operates on the assumption that truth and justice emerge from the clash of ideas. The preceding example also shows how the clash of ideas and disagreements can lead to more workable decisions in the online classroom. The instructor was able to get Richard to "own" the decision to temper his communication because the conflict was posed as a problem in need of a solution, not a conflict in need of resolution. If the instructor's decision to stop all sharing of personal moral viewpoints had been imposed, Richard and other students would have felt disenfranchised. They would have most certainly carried around increased feelings of isolation and resentments about the decision that could have interfered with future performance, cooperation and decisions in the electronic classroom. The ultimate decision got the task completed and it strengthened relationships. In addition, Richard

felt a part of the decision and was more likely to respect it. He realized that he was part of a real—though virtual—community.

3. *Help students realize that feelings exist online.* Here I must emphasize that I am not talking about allowing online students to flame each other. It is crucial that feelings are communicated productively online. I am talking about opportunities to express and explain feelings through respectful language. Online conflicts, if responded to effectively, can be positive opportunities for getting feelings out in a medium that is mostly assumed to be impersonal. Dealing with feelings shows students the human element that is always present in the online environment. As the previous example shows, if the energy of a feeling such as anger can be channeled into a positive communication framework, the feelings can be used to find creative solutions and more complete human relationships.

4. *Promote confidence in online learning.* There is always uncertainty in a person when things really get difficult. The first serious argument with another student or instructor is a major event. This is especially true in online learning situations where the phenomenon of flaming suggests that communication becomes more extreme and impulsive. But the confidence that follows a well-managed online conflict can be extremely valuable to learning. It is often those educational encounters that avoid conflict that are ultimately the most insecure and unproductive because they remain untested. Both online students in the preceding example felt a new sureness, a new security, in their working relationship. Their online relationship was tested by conflict, and they had the opportunity to develop trust and confidence by learning how to communicate successfully through those conflicts. They ultimately recognized the value of the experience and the important learning that took place.

Of course, a positive attitude is the first step to responding effectively to online conflict. Faculty and students need to begin seeing conflict as creative and productive. The second step is to recognize that online conflict comes in several types.

Types of Online Conflict

Conflict is a pervasive part of all human relationships, including those in the electronic classroom. In fact, some philosophers have suggested that it is what makes us human. All humans are different and conflict is just a reflection of that natural condition. To eliminate conflict online would mean eliminating its most human element. Without differences, online learning would not be an interpersonal activity.

But in order to respond effectively through online conflict, faculty and students also need to recognize that not all disagreement is the same. There are three basic types of online conflict:

1. *There is conflict over facts or interpretations.* This kind of disagreement reflects differing views over the content and expectations of an online course. They are disagreements over fact. People can disagree over the fact that Columbus landed in the Western Hemisphere in 1492 (which can easily be confirmed or disconfirmed) or they can disagree over meaning-- whether he "discovered" America at all (which is a matter of interpretation). The most important question to ask yourself when dealing with this type of online conflict is: What level of conflict are you disagreeing about—fact or meaning? It makes a difference. Your syllabus may say that students are required to interact in the online class, but what does *interaction* mean? Is a student who always responds to other student comments with short statements such as "I agree" actually interacting? And what is "correct grammar" online? Should online discussion be evaluated by the same grammatical standards as more formal online assignments like term papers or case studies? Or are online discussions, although textual, more like conversations? In addition, what does "page" mean online? Is a page one screen or is it a traditional page in length? These kinds of small conflicts over facts and interpretations can be very disruptive in an online class until they are discussed and clarified. In fact, flaming is often the consequence of different interpretations of words.

One fundamental online conflict over facts or interpretation can be about what an online class is. Generally speaking, an online course can be accessed anywhere and anytime, and makes use of computer technology to deliver student learning at flexible times and places. But some online classes do not require any attendance or participation—resembling "correspondence courses" more than interactive experiences that include the faculty member and other students. Many online students enter programs with their own definition of what an online course is; thus, there is an immediate need to clarify the nature of the course and the roles of faculty members and students.

2. *There is conflict over online roles and identities.* This kind of disagreement particularly reflects differing perspectives over the roles of online instructors. Cues in traditional educational settings reinforce social differences. An instructor lecturing at the front of a classroom or meeting a student in an office is a reminder of status differences. Online technologies

weaken social differences apparent in face to face communication. Online instructors are not awarded authority or expertise by students simply because instructors look the part. All online messages have an equal status to a certain degree because they look alike. The only thing that can set them apart is their content, or what William James might call their "cash value." Without the "halo effect" of status, the competence and ability of the online instructor are in question from the beginning of class and are only earned through the quality of messages and how informative they are. While traditional students in a regular classroom might tend to accept the instructor's viewpoints as authority, online students tend to more readily question and challenge instructor opinions.

Consequently, many online conflicts about roles and identities focus on whether an instructor is considered informed or uninformed or are centered on who has what kind of authority with a given topic. Being labeled by students as informed is an important step in defining your position as the online instructor, but that is balanced against similar needs of many online students. Many online students are working adults in established careers. They have learned enormously from certain important work and other life experiences. They have learned how to learn a great deal in ways other than taking courses. They are the "experts" in many topics. This experience needs to be recognized and utilized by the online instructor. That is why many instructors prefer to identify themselves as *facilitators*, understanding that online conflicts around power relationships can be understood as struggles over such identities and roles. Stewart and colleagues (2007) say that communication is often about the "negotiation-of-selves."

3. *There is conflict over values.* Online instructors recognize that online classes are part of social organizations as well as places where people accomplish individual and collective tasks. Over a time period, most organizations develop a culture that strongly affects the way people view their place of work, its management and its primary purposes. Although *culture in organizations* is defined as the common values of both managers and employees, cultural values are not simply imposed. They are developed over time. There can be disagreements over organizational values, such as over the level of expectations of all members of the staff and regarding what *service to customers* means. In fact, conflict over cultural values may be necessary. Communication and human relations in organizations with well-defined, positive cultural values are nearly always better than in those that pay little attention to the values of the organization. There is value in communicating through conflict about organizational values. But they are most effectively dealt with in a structured way where there is an opportunity for mutual respect, learning and maintaining interpersonal relationships.

As suggested above, the values of various online programs differ. For example, is *education* a value? Many working adults who enter online programs may not really want the education—they want what the education provides for them in better jobs, moving up the career ladder and the ability to communicate ideas. But are those the values of the particular online programs they enter? If a student enters your class with the above values, and you expect an "intellectual life," than there might be a conflict over values.

Ultimately, the main point is to know your conflict. But whatever the type of conflict, the next step in responding effectively is knowing what to do, or knowing what *not* to do—reacting.

Reacting to Online Conflict

Going back to the beginning of this chapter and the distinction made between *reacting* and *responding*, the following ways of dealing with online conflict can be identified as "reactive." A reactive approach does not see that whenever there is disagreement, there are always four elements to the conflict: (1) *you*, (2) *the other person*, (3) *the topic* and (4) *the climate*. Imagine a circle where each one of the conflict elements makes up one quarter of the circle. In order for the circle to be whole, it must include every element.

The first three elements of conflict are easy to understand. The *you* of a conflict is anyone who deals with the second part of conflict—*other people*. The *topic*, of course, is the subject of what you and others are talking about. The *climate* of a conflict can be the physical environment and objects (on the phone, face to face, in the kitchen or office, on the computer, the temperature of the room) but also the emotional level of the topic.

Virginia Satir (1972) defines the reactive styles in these four ways:

1. *"Placating" is when we ignore yourself in online conflict.* Placating is an example of denying that a conflict exists. It is unresponsive because it fails to acknowledge disagreement. It avoids the conflict by using statements that terminate "talk" about the conflict before the discussion has thoroughly developed. It writes in generalities and avoids specifics. When online instructors or students placate a conflict, they do not directly accept their responsibility. Often online placators lurk in the background of the class, simply observing and keeping their opinions to themselves.

2. *"Pouncing" is when we try to ignore or eliminate the other person in the online conflict.* Pouncing or blaming another person as a way of driving him or her away from the disagreement. It is when you want the other person

to placate. Flaming, the online equal of pouncing, is often based on the belief that your view is the only "right" one. Some signs of flaming include name calling, rejection, hostile questioning, hostile joking and accusations. Flaming is an example of controlling an online conflict. It is unresponsive because it fails to acknowledge the other person's opinions. When people flame, they tend to communicate with an air of superiority and intimidation. They can run the gamut from "deadly quiet" to sarcastic and "loud". Often they type in ALL CAPS which is interpreted as yelling online. Pouncers—online flamers—are so intent on being right that they do not really read what other online students are writing, even when asked a direct question.

3. *"Distracting" is when we try to change the subject of the online conflict.* Distracting assumes that if you change the subject, the conflict will go away. It doesn't. The clearest sign of distracting is an abrupt change of the topic. One example is when the online student substitutes social chat for substantive responses to discussion questions. This conflict usually centers on the person's role as an online student. Many people enter online learning programs expecting a "correspondence course" experience. Often, what they find is an educational experience with required social interaction and expectations for contributing to the understanding of a subject matter. If an online student is not prepared for such a role (which is the conflict), he or she often responds with social chat or low participation. The online instructor must recognize the distracting nature of this behavior and encourage the student to contribute by asking specific questions that will move the student forward, or by addressing the issue through personal messages. But the conflict must be recognized. Online instructors need to be prepared for angry responses when such a student is pushed to contribute more significantly or when the issue is raised through a personal message. Such distracting is an example of diverting an underlying conflict.

4. *"Computing" is when we try to ignore the emotional climate of the online conflict.* Computing is an example of not only ignoring the human potential of online learning, but further dehumanizing an online conflict. It is unresponsive because it fails to acknowledge the feelings of a real person on the other end of the computer. It sees the online environment as simply technical, not interpersonal. When people compute, they tend to remain impersonal. They use jargon and technical language. Often they only want to deal with "the cold, hard facts." They are so intent on being detached that they often talk in the third person and show little awareness of audience and personal voice. Instead of seeing what others in the class are up to, and writing more as dialogue, they remain abstract.

Conclusion

The most effective way to communicate through conflict is by *responding*. It is communication that "responds" to all four parts of the conflict—you, the other, the topic and the climate. It responds to feelings and "stands up for its own rights". It responds to the student by asking about and listening for feelings and attitudes, and it "sticks to the topic." Finally, it responds to the emotional climate of the conflict by recognizing that feelings have a place online.

I conclude this chapter with some suggestions offered by Sillars and colleagues (1982) that can be directly applied to the online class. Responding effectively to online conflict can be practiced by using certain kinds of interpersonal and supportive statements. These include:

- *Using descriptive language.* Statements about observable events and behaviors related to the conflict should be non-evaluative. For example, you might write a note such as the following to a student's personal mailbox: "I feel that you were trying to be humorous with this statement, but it can come across as sarcastic to some people. What do you think?" Or if you are dealing with late assignments: "My records indicate that I did not receive your weekly summary assignment. Is that correct?" Descriptive language tends to be tentative.

- *Setting limits.* Statements should explicitly qualify the nature and extent of the conflict, as well as set clear boundaries. If an online student has been disruptive, you might first make a comment in the main meeting room letting all students know the expectations of higher education and of the class. This step allows the student to save face while being informed of important limits. If this does not work, then you can telephone the student or send a message via his or her personal mailbox. The syllabus is the most important place to lay out clear boundaries for the class, particularly regarding tone, student responsibilities, quantity and quality of participation, cheating, grading and late work.

- *Offering support.* Statements should express understanding, acceptance or positive regard for the other person. I often send messages to the main meeting telling students how much I appreciate the tone of their online communication. In this way, I attempt to establish some cultural norms for the class. I also address process issues as well as content in my feedback.

- *Emphasizing commonalties and relationship reminders.* Statements should comment on common ground. I often send a message to the main meeting where I will say something like the following: "As a member of this class, I'm feeling uncomfortable with the tone of the present conversation. I'm feeling that some people could interpret it as sarcastic. What does everyone else feel?" In this message, I emphasize our common ground as members of the class and as human beings with feelings. I remind online students that conflict exists within a broader context of mutual commitment, respect, understanding and learning.

• *Initiating problem solving.* Statements should initiate mutual consideration of solutions. If there is a conflict between two students, I contact them both privately either through their private mailboxes or telephone. I attempt to describe what I see and ask them how the problem can be solved.

• *Fractionating.* Break conflicts down from one big mass into several smaller pieces. Stay very specific. Do not interpret a poor use of words as a value conflict. Attempt to address the conflict by contacting the student through his or her personal mailbox or telephone before it emerges in the main meeting.

• *Defusing.* Continually ask yourself: "How well am I responding to conflict?" Defusing is reading notes carefully, identifying areas of agreement, and maintaining a positive tone. By listening carefully and communicating your own values cautiously, you can help create a sense of trust and mutual respect for differences in the online classroom.

But remember, most of all, you can respond most effectively to online conflict by remembering conflict is an important learning opportunity.

References

Satir, V. (1972). *Peoplemaking.* Palo Alto, CA: Science and Behavior Books.

Sillers, A.L., Coletti, S.F., Parry, D. and Rogers, M.A. (1982). Coding verbal conflict tactics: nonverbal and perceptual correlates of the 'avoidance-distributive-integrative' distinction. *Human Communication Research*, 9, Fall, 83-95.

Sproull, L. and Kiesler, S. (1991*). Connections: New Ways of Working in the Networked Organization.* Cambridge, MA: The MIT Press.

Stewart, J., Zediker, K.E. & Witteborn, S. (2007). *Together: Communicating Interpersonally: A Social Construction Approach.* New York: Oxford University Press

Chapter 11

MAKING SENSE OF IT ALL

GIVING & GETTING ONLINE COURSE FEEDBACK

by Ken White

In 1987, Arthur W. Chickering and Zelda Gamson published the *Seven Principles for Good Practice* distilled from decades of research on learning in higher education. Principle number four states: *"Good practice in undergraduate education gives prompt feedback."*

Prompt feedback recognizes that undergraduate students need to know what they know and do not know in order to focus their learning. Students need help in assessing existing knowledge and performance, as well as opportunities to get suggestions for improvement. They need to reflect on what they have learned, what they still need to learn, and how to evaluate the learning process.

Feedback is even more critical in the online environment, where students may feel isolated and detached. More than traditional students, online students need appropriate feedback on performance because learning in the online medium is complicated by the disconnection of electronic textual communication. Devoid of the environmental and nonverbal signals available in face to face contact, the online classroom requires effective feedback in order to alleviate some of this disconnection and to reduce feelings of isolation in the online student.

Online instructors also need feedback. They need help assessing existing objectives, teaching styles, methods and ways of evaluating. They need to reflect on past practice, ways of improving and how to meaningfully evaluate the online teaching process.

Online instructors need to give and to get constructive feedback. Consequently, this chapter will discuss some of the issues facing online faculty members when they try to give and get feedback to achieve their instructional goals, looking at the major characteristics of feedback and its various roles. The chapter will also look at an alternative tool available to help online faculty members get constructive feedback and valuable information from their students. It will describe the *Small Group Instructional Dialogue* process or SGID and its applicability to the online classroom.

Giving Constructive Online Feedback

For the purposes of this discussion, a distinction will be made between three characteristics of constructive online feedback. *Formative* feedback modifies a student's thinking or behavior for the purpose of learning. By influencing thought and behavior, it can best be seen as motivational. It encourages students to continue down the road they are traveling or to consider changing direction. For example, online students need to be encouraged to do the following:

- Stay the course when they are on the right path
- Modify their thinking or approach when necessary
- Ask questions
- Participate
- Stay on the subject

Summative feedback assesses how well a student accomplishes a task or achieves a result for the purpose of grading. Online students need summative feedback. They want to know where they stand with relation to their classmates and, in the case of many adult and online learners, where they stand with relation to their employer's tuition rebate policy. If the student is receiving regular summative feedback, there are few surprises when final grades are given.

Formative and summative feedback illustrates how online feedback can provide a continuous flow of information that helps students to shape the learning process while it is happening and to fulfill their ultimate expectations. The following characteristics should be considered in providing such comprehensive feedback. Feedback should be:

1. *Multi-dimensional*. Covers a variety of areas such as content, process, outcomes and other issues.
2. *Non-evaluative*. Provides objective information about the student's work; allows the student to step back from his or her work and personally acknowledge strengths and weaknesses.
3. *Reflective*. Delivers information in a way that encourages the student to recognize areas for improvement.

4. *Student Controlled.* Gives the student choices about how they respond to the information.
5. *Timely.* Offers the students immediate feedback after completing the assignment or activity.
6. *Specific.* Describes specific observations and makes specific recommendations for the student's consideration.

Supportive feedback is also crucial for online students. In a now-famous essay, Jack Gibb described the characteristics of supportive communication and of its opposite, defensive-arousing communication, and thereby as well established the underlying principles of constructive online feedback. Gibb (1961) concluded that communication creates feelings of discomfort and defensiveness when either its content, or the way in which it is presented, makes people feel that they are being:

- Judged
- Manipulated or controlled inappropriately
- Subjected to cold, impersonal treatment
- Treated as a relatively interchangeable person

Gibb recognized that feedback could either support or attack a person's sense of worth and security. The difference between defense-arousing and supportive online feedback may be how the messages are communicated. His observations suggest some other possible "best practices" for giving online feedback. Online instructors need to practice specific skills when giving constructive feedback to students.

Online feedback should:

1. *Focus on specific behavior rather than on the online student.* It is important that online instructors refer to what a student *does* rather than to what they think he or she *is*. They might say that an online student "participated too much in a class meeting" rather than that he or she is "dominating." To be told that one is dominating is not as useful as to be told that "in the discussion that just took place, you did not appear to understand what the other students were communicating and they seemed to have felt forced to accept your arguments." The former approach implies a negative personality trait; the latter one allows for the possibility of change.

Like everyone else, it is easier for online students to change specific behaviors rather than personalities. Describing one's reactions to behavior allows students to judge the behavior for themselves and to decide how to use it or not use it. The goal is to focus on specific observations, not on inferences.

In addition, by avoiding psychological language or speculating on motives, online instructors reduce the need for students to respond defensively (or flame). It encourages online students to make sense of their own behavior.

Focusing on specific behaviors also allows online instructors to share information rather than give advice. By sharing information, an online instructor gives the student responsibility for helping to decide if the feedback is appropriate and in accordance with important goals and needs of the online classroom. When instructors give advice, they can take away important degrees of freedom and discourage taking responsibility. Sharing information puts the focus on developing alternatives, not merely on accepting solutions.

2. *Take the needs of the online student into account.* Feedback is counter productive when it serves only instructional needs and fails to consider the needs of the student on the other end of the computer. Constructive feedback is given to help—not because it makes faculty feel better or gives them a psychological advantage. It should focus on the kind and amount of information the individual online student can assimilate and use.

3. *Direct your feedback toward behavior the online student can change.* Frustration and aggressive resistance are only increased when an online student is reminded of some shortcoming over which he or she has no control. Attribution theory states that the willingness to change depends on a person's ability to see his or her own efforts contribute to success. Success must be perceived as caused, at least in a substantial part, by one's own efforts. As teachers, we know that students who believe their efforts influence their achievement are more likely to learn that are students who believe that learning depends on teachers or something else beyond their own control. It works the same for online students

4. *Help online students to "own" the feedback.* Constructive feedback is most useful when it is given in the kind of communication climate that encourages the online student to actively seek feedback. Constructive online feedback encourages students to be responsible for identifying their strengths and weaknesses and ways of enhancing online performance. One student may concentrate on participating in online discussions more effectively while another may look at how to improve essays. Constructive feedback is often solicited as well as offered.

5. *Give timely online feedback.* Constructive feedback is most useful immediately after the observed behavior. The online student more readily understands how the information relates to his or her intentions, and thus is in a position to be more accepting of alternative patterns of behavior for trying to solve problems. To the degree that there is a delay in the communication of

significant information, there is forgetting, and often what is forgotten is a particular factor that would promote the necessary change in behavior.

6. *Check your online feedback for clarity.* Having the online student respond to feedback gives you, the instructor, an opportunity to check the accuracy of your feedback.

7. *Consider your online feedback as part of an ongoing relationship.* Constructive feedback opens the way up to a relationship with an online student built on communication, growth and concern. Through such learning relationships, everyone becomes senders and receivers of valuable feedback and experiences.

Getting Constructive Online Feedback

In addition to giving constructive feedback, online instructors need to appreciate and use various sources of information to improve online teaching and learning. As an online instructor since 1992, I have learned that any source of information for improving online teaching and learning offers important but limited insights. While online administrators evaluate course loads, enrollment factors and other long-range considerations, the online instructor that can best explain the reasons for instructional decisions. Online faculty peers can appraise instructional objectives and the currency of subject matter, but it is really online students who are in a better position to comment on classroom teaching skills, course difficulty and online instructor-student interaction.

Consequently, the clearest picture of an online teaching situation emerges when various perspectives are solicited. In order for online teaching to be effective, it needs to include the feedback of student opinions. A lack of such feedback significantly affects the ability of online faculty to make their instructions and assignments clear and meaningful, and open to productive student interpretations. In addition, online teaching and learning are about relationships. A lack of online student feedback significantly affects the quality of the teacher-student communication, making it much more difficult to coordinate meaning.

When interested in online student perceptions, a good place to start is with the *Small Group Instructional Dialogue* (SGID). As an alternative procedure, SGIDs offer the major benefit of taking place mid-way through a course, thus giving the instructor the opportunity to make changes to the course before it ends and before students complete any end-of-the-course evaluations. The procedure involves *structured* questions that ask online students in a given course to describe what helps them learn and how improvements can be made. Pioneered for traditional onsite courses at the University of Washington by D. Joseph Clark (Clark & Bekey, 1979), the SGID has developed into an effective means for evaluating teaching effectiveness.

(I retain the popular and communicative acronym of SGID, but I focus on the dialogical nature of the process rather than on its "diagnostic" or problem-solving features and thus refer to the SGID as the *Small Group Instructional Dialogue*.)

As I explained in an earlier article (White, 1991) the original onsite process takes approximately 25 minutes of class time and requires a facilitator, usually a trained colleague, to obtain information directly from students. On a prearranged day, in the absence of the instructor, the facilitator asks students to form groups of 4-6 people. Small groups are important because they serve to place extreme student opinions within the context of group consensus, increase validity and better reflect the complexity of the learning environment.

Small groups each select a recorder and come to consensus on two main questions:

1. *What helps you learn in this class?*
2. *What improvements would you like to see and how would you make those improvements?*

Following ten minutes of discussion, the groups report 2-3 ideas on each question to the entire class. A student volunteer records the comments. The facilitator summarizes the groups' ideas on the board, paraphrasing, questioning and clarifying the information until students reach a consensus and the facilitator demonstrates a clear understanding of the student viewpoint.

In order to introduce the approach to instructors, to prepare them for the kind of feedback they will receive, and to help them respond to their students about the feedback, SGIDs usually involve three distinct stages: a pre-SGID conversation, the SGID itself, and a post-SGID discussion. A pre-SGID meeting with the faculty member clarifies what the process can and cannot do, explains how it differs from other forms of feedback, and obtains knowledge about course goals, class activities and other matters that expedite the in-class part of the process. During the post-SGID conversation with the instructor, the task of the facilitator is to respect student opinions, and highlight themes and explanations that integrate student and instructor perceptions. The conversation moves to strategies for change and what the instructor can say to students when returning to the classroom and talking about the SGID results.

SGIDs are especially useful in student-centered and group-oriented classrooms. The SGID is more personal than individual student ratings and allows students to hear what other students are thinking. The process emphasizes that students have a role in shaping their own instruction and learning. This chapter suggests that the SGID process can easily be adapted to online education. Online mid-course feedback can be the basis of a productive course by promoting productive student-teacher communication (Bruning, 2005). It can become an integral part of an effective online course. In the following section, I will describe the adaptation and application of the SGID procedure to online courses.

The Online Small Group Instructional Dialogue

At the beginning of an online course, I introduce the idea of a SGID mid-course feedback in the syllabus. The procedure begins with a call for a student volunteer in the syllabus section that outlines the third week of the five or six week course (week five of a traditional ten work course). The syllabus informs the online students that they should send a message to the volunteer where they will list: (1) three areas that are working well in this course and (2) three ways to improve the class. The volunteer will then combine all of the messages—verbatim and unedited—and send them to me.

In these pre-SGID instructions, I ask that no names be attached to this information so that all participants remain anonymous. Of course, I am not able to distinguish the volunteer's comments from others. I explain how the information will be used to make changes for the last two weeks of the course and for future courses. I conclude with comments about how much I appreciate their honesty and participation. I also point out that the students will receive a formal end-of-the-course evaluation form from the university administration. I encourage them to wait until after they have completed the SGID mid-course feedback and have received my responses before they send in the official student evaluation to the administration. The mid-course feedback usually responds to many online student questions and concerns.

At any rate, it is important for online students to understand what the process can and cannot do and how it differs from the formal end-of-the-course student evaluations. The process is voluntary, anonymous and confidential for the online students. Students are not required to respond; if they do, they will remain anonymous; and only the online instructor will see the information—it is not intended for administrators. Because SGID mid-course feedback is not a formal evaluation, it encourages a safe environment for online student feedback.

The strength of information from online SGID feedback for students is that it can be used to change things immediately, even in a five-week course. For example, in one online mid-course feedback procedure, students in a Managerial Ethics and Responsibility course responded that they would prefer to locate related articles from the Internet rather than read assigned articles (that were slightly outdated) from the text. The instructor was able to respond by allowing the students to locate Internet articles for the last two weeks of class. This particular information resulted in positive comments in the formal end-of-the-course evaluations and in a number of good articles that the online instructor was later able to use in other classes.

After introducing and describing the procedure in the syllabus, I upload a reminder message in the third week of class asking for a volunteer. Typically, two or three students respond either in the main meeting room or through the instructor's personal mailbox. I then send the following message to the main meeting for everyone to read:

To:	**MbXXX Mgt592**
From:	**[Your name]**
Subject:	**Mid-course Feedback**
Written:	**Tues Feb 17 at 9:04am**

Thanks for volunteering, Joe. I usually do this "first come, first serve," so if it's OK with the rest of the class, you're it.

Everyone else will send you his or her comments by this Wednesday. These comments should include 2-3 ideas about what's working well in this class and 2-3 areas that need improvement. Like in all constructive feedback, the positive comments should come first.

Remember not to send suggestions to the open forum where names can be associated with specific comments.

Please compile the feedback verbatim under the two categories— WHAT'S WORKING WELL and AREAS FOR IMPROVEMENT (in that order)—and don't do any editing. The compilation should be done anonymously with no names attached to any information.

Then send the compilation to my personal mailbox. I'll add my responses and send all the information back to the open forum verbatim for all students to read.

Thanks again, Joe, for volunteering and to everyone for participating. I appreciate it.

The online students then send their responses to the following two questions to the student volunteer's (Joe's) personal mailbox:

1. What helps you learn in this course?
2. What improvements would you like and how would you
   suggest they be made?

After the online students send their comments to the volunteer, the task is to compile the comments verbatim and without any editing. Seeking themes is an important part of SGID feedback, but it is also important to look for differences and areas of disagreement. Online students always see the course and instructor from differing perspectives. Some say the reading load for the course is too great, while others counter that it is not. These kinds of comparisons are useful for both the online students and the instructor because they contextualize individual student perceptions and insights about the course and test them in a public forum. If everyone does not share a statement, the instructor and the student who made the comment can better judge the statement's significance. Consequently, the compilation doesn't necessarily summarize the information but presents it as "raw data" in order to maintain the integrity of individual statements.

A typical example of a mid-course feedback compilation looks like the following:

To:	**[Your name]**
From:	**Joe Smith**
Subject:	**SGID Assessment**
Written:	**Thurs Feb 19 at 7:45pm**

Here's the compilation of the comments I received from the other students in the class.

WHAT'S WORKING WELL:

1. I think the course content is excellent. There is a good mix of the text material and lecture information. The added feature of classmate input really rounds out the material. Using a problem from your current work area is a nice touch.

2. I was a little skeptical of this online format because of the indirect interaction. I have been totally pleased with the outcome. I think the interaction has been excellent and very beneficial.

3. I feel that the class syllabus was well laid out and was very easy to follow. I knew exactly what was expected of me and on what day it was expected.

4. The instructor had some good assignments that helped me to understand the point he was trying to convey to us. Also the points of the other classmates helped to broaden my outlook on issues.

5. The class discussions are great! The opportunity to converse with one another on each lecture is a learning experience indeed.

6. I like the exercises too. These provide a chance for us to learn about ourselves.

7. I like the fact that I can sit here in front of my computer, dressed any way I please, at any hour of the day I please and "attend" class.

8. I really liked the additional information the instructor provided outside the lectures.

9. The consistency of the assignment schedule each week. This helps because we are all working individuals and we can schedule around the weekly class schedule.

10. The response part of the assignment. When we respond it ensures that we read each other's views on the question and that we compare each other's views.

11. The chapters that are combined each week seem to compliment each other and flow well with the syllabus and work retrospectively as the weeks go by.

AREAS FOR IMPROVEMENT:

1. Group discussions that require consensus. I don't believe that we can do this effectively with the random way we individually handle our online sessions.

2. Whether needed or not, the class should be aware of the online etiquette at the very beginning of class. This could be supported through an assignment.

3. The use of the first syllabus as a guide and then not reiterating this in the following weeks. I was and still have to go back and forth between the initial syllabus and comparing it to the assignments. This may be an organizational problem of mine.

4. I would have liked to have seen an example of a well-written short report.

5. Personally, I need to organize my time more efficiently in order to balance the demands of my family, my full-time job, my part-time job and this course.

6. When we need feedback from instructor, please follow through with it.

7. If people cannot send in assignments due to various situations, please have them contact the instructor to inform other classmates. Our feedback sometimes relies on individual input and we wonder why we haven't heard anything. It holds up the other students at times.

8. The only thing I can think of that hasn't gone well was the exercise to reach a layoff consensus. The exercise was interesting, but I think the online interaction system was stretched just a little too far. The communication sequence was tough to maintain and sometimes the timing of answers was out of sync.

It is then important to respond to student's feedback as soon as possible. A sample of the kinds of responses I send back to online students is below:

To:	MbXXX MGT592
From:	[Your name]
Subject:	Mid-course Feedback Responses
Written:	Fri Feb 20 at 8:10am

Below are responses to your course comments. I follow specific comments with my responses enclosed in ***asterisks***.

3. The use of the first syllabus as a guide and then not reiterating this in the following weeks. I was and I still have to go back and forth between the initial syllabus and comparing it to the assignments. This may be an organizational problem of mine.

No, I see your point. What I can begin to do is reiterate the relevant parts of the syllabus at the beginning of each week's lecture. Thanks.

4. I would have liked to see an example of a well-written short report.

You're right! I will send an example of an excellent short report to the"MbXXX Reports" branch meeting right away.

5. Personally, I need to organize my time more efficiently in order to balance the demands of my family, my full-time job, my part-time job and this course.

Don't we all! Online classes are a commitment.

6. When we need feedback from instructor, please follow through with it.

I'm assuming that I do. Would someone give me a more specific example?

7. If people cannot send in assignments due to various situations, please have them contact the instructor to inform other classmates. Our feedback sometimes relies on the individual input and we wonder why we haven't heard anything. It holds up the other students at times.

I do send personal messages to students who have not sent their work in, but it's a good idea to suggest that they also inform the class. I need to encourage more personal responsibility in this area

8. The only thing I can think of that hasn't gone well was the exercise to reach a layoff consensus. The exercise was interesting, but I think the online interaction system was stretched just a little too far. The communication sequence was tough to maintain and sometimes the timing of answers was out of sync.

Reaching consensus online is particularly challenging. But I think you did a very good job. In addition, it's not so much that you reach a perfect consensus, but that you learn something on the way. But I'll keep your point in mind. Maybe I can do a better job of summarizing the level of consensus along the way. Thanks.

Finally, there is an optional step that can be added to the online SGID process and better encourages the consensual and dialogical elements of the procedure. At the point where the volunteer is to send me the raw data, I set up a special meeting or forum where the volunteer displays the combined information. I assure the students that I will not participate or lurk in this meeting in order to maintain the confidential and anonymous nature of the process. Each online student can then read the data and express their agreement or disagreement with each item. As a consequence, the online students get the opportunity to have a dialogue about the information and to reach a genuine consensus. It is after this dialogue that the volunteer then sends me the information.

Benefits and Limitations of SGID Mid-course Feedback

Like other sources of information, SGID feedback offers benefits and limitations. Based on online student comments, mid-course feedback is successful and associated with several advantages. They are:

1. The process builds on a positive foundation of what works well.
2. It offers different categories than standardized ratings.
3. Its mid-course timing allows instructors to make changes during the same online class.
4. Its feedback contains specific suggestions on how to make those changes.

SGID mid-course feedback is especially useful in online classrooms because it is more personal than individual student ratings and allows students to read what other students are thinking. Its group orientation builds interpersonal associations and reinforces the online learner's expectations for sharing experiences and for developing social cohesion. Basically, SGID feedback emphasizes that online students have a role in shaping their own instruction and learning.

On the other hand, SGID feedback has its limits. If used as a summative procedure for hiring or firing online faculty, the process can stifle open communication with students, not to mention creating extraordinary faculty anxiety and distrust of the process. Students usually share honest information and constructive perspectives about their courses because it is designed to help faculty improve their teaching. When mid-course information is used otherwise, students can become reluctant to share opinions they feel threaten their instructors. Consequently, maintaining SGID feedback as a formative process—voluntary, anonymous and confidential—helps to encourage open communication and meaningful online student feedback.

Mentoring Faculty with SGID Feedback

The SGID feedback can also be used to help mentor beginning online faculty and can be an important part of a formative faculty training or development program. I often consult with colleges about how to facilitate SGIDs and how to institutionalize the process. New and seasoned online instructors often need to learn about specific aspects of their initial teaching. One major advantage of SGID feedback is that the questions can be tailored to respond to the concrete needs of online instructors. For example, a recently mentored online instructor wanted to know if his students were gaining a thorough understanding of the dynamics between theory and business practice in class discussions. A seasoned online instructor wanted information on course structure and the incorporation of current news items into the curriculum. In both of these situations, I worked with the instructors to frame specific feedback questions that would get directly at their concerns. The flexibility of the SGID feedback procedure offered opportunities to respond to the mentored and seasoned instructors' concerns by changing generic questions in order to address more immediate needs.

Soon after the SGID feedback, I telephone the online instructor to discuss the information, answer questions, explain comments and offer alternative interpretations of apparent contradictions. During this phase, the task is to acknowledge online student perspectives. Though the intent is not to persuade the online faculty member to agree with the students, it is to highlight themes and explanations that integrate student and instructor perceptions.

Occasionally, online students flame an instructor and write negative comments in a harsh way. In these cases, I emphasize that student comments are only one perspective. I try to encourage a cooperative venture in problem-solving with the online instructor by sharing my own relevant teaching experiences and suggesting where online students may be "coming from." In this manner, I try to promote reflection on the issues, and not just on the students' words. The conversation can then move to strategies for constructive change.

Conclusion

Just as there is no simple system for evaluating the quality of online learning, there is no simple system for evaluating the quality of online teaching. However, by thinking carefully about the purposes of feedback, and by crafting multiple methods of giving and getting online feedback, one can devise effective and constructive approaches. The process of thinking about online feedback focuses attention on the practice of good online teaching and helps to create another educational culture in which teaching and learning are highly valued.

SGID online feedback can make a positive contribution to online instructional improvement and student learning. As a formative, summative and supportive process for online teaching and learning, SGID feedback can be a trusted form of student information. It can be a catalyst for change in a variety of online teaching and learning settings.

References

Bruning, K. (2005). Implementing a midcourse feedback procedure in the online learning environment. *http://www.itdl.org/Journal/Jun_05/article04.htm*

Clark, D.J. & Bekey, J. (1979). Use of small groups in instructional evaluation. *POD Quarterly*, 1 (2), 87-95.

Chickering, A.W, & Gamson, Z.F. (1987). *Seven Principles for Good Practice in Undergraduate Education: Faculty Inventory*. Racine, WI: The Johnson Foundation, Inc.

Gibb, J. (1961). Defensive communication. *Journal of Communication*, 11, 1341-148.

White, K. (1991). Small group instructional diagnosis. *Adult Assessment Forum*, 1, number 3.

Index

Printed in the United States
211992BV00001B/7/P